THE OFFICIAL
MANCHESTER UNITED
100
GREATEST
PLAYERS

PUBLISHER'S ACKNOWLEDGEMENT

Carlton Books Limited would like to thank the Publishers and Editors of *Manchester United Magazine* for their kind permission to use the poll of Manchester United supporters, which they conducted, as the basis for this book.

AUTHOR'S NOTE

It was obvious when I first saw the list of the 100 players featured in this book that, to my mind, many great players had been omitted and so, firstly, I would like to apologise to them and also to those who may well feel they should have figured a little higher in the pecking order!

My brief, though, was to recall the careers and characters of those voted for by the readers of the Manchester United Magazine, and it soon emerged that the modern players have fared particularly well. You will note that virtually the entire present-day squad is nominated as a Great, which is perhaps a reflection of the general readership age.

I have no problem with that, except to say that I am conscious that if we are talking Manchester United history here, where are the likes of Billy Meredith, a remarkable Welsh winger whose League career covered 29 years and some 700 games, or Joe Spence, who was so popular between the wars that the crowd used to shout: "Give it to Joe"?

Then there was Harry Stafford, the legendary captain whose dog played a part saving the club from bankruptcy in 1901 and who also became a United director. For every player mentioned here, I could name another of equal merit.

But I have certainly enjoyed what – for me – has been a trip down memory lane, for I have either watched, reported on, or interviewed every single one of the nominated Greats. So with this in mind I would like to dedicate the book to them, and at the same time pass on my thanks to John Doherty, a Busby Babe whose omission as a Great particularly embarrasses me, and who helped me fill in a few blanks from his rich memory of his playing days.

My thanks, also, to my editor, Vanessa Daubney, for her help and encouragement.

David Meek
July 2001

THIS IS A CARLTON BOOK

First published in 2001

Copyright © Manchester United 2001
Text and design © Carlton Books Limited 2001

Manufactured and distributed by
Carlton Books Limited
20 Mortimer Street
London W1T 3JW

A CIP catalogue record for this book is available from the British Library

ISBN 0-233-99963-9

Project Editor: Vanessa Daubney
Project Art Direction: Mark Lloyd
Design: Neil Wallace
Jacket Design: Steve Lynn
Picture Research: Daffydd Bynon
Production: Lisa French

Printed and bound in Italy

THE OFFICIAL
MANCHESTER UNITED
100
GREATEST
PLAYERS

David Meek

CARLTON
BOOKS

CONTENTS

FOREWORD

I went to my first match in 1968, when I was seven or eight years old, and at that time it was the classic United team with George Best, Bobby Charlton and Denis Law, all of whom would have to be in my list of great United players. But I also look back with regret at not having been able to see the 1950s Busby Babes and so compare them to the later teams. From what people tell me, I'm sure it would be a tough job.

Even so, it's difficult to choose one particular player above all the others. Apart from Charlton and Law, I think Ryan Giggs, who has been a phenomenal servant to the club, is a great, great player and I am delighted that David Beckham's talent has led to his becoming England captain.

Of course, in recent years, Eric Cantona has probably made the biggest impact at the club, as you will see from the results of the fans' poll upon which this book is based. But my favourite player has to be George Best. He was an idol to me and, when he left United, I was devastated and lost interest in football for a while because of it. So, for me, separating George Best and Eric Cantona is a hard task.

I've enjoyed so many great times watching United, but one of my fondest moments is when we won the European Cup Winners' Cup against Barcelona in Rotterdam in 1991. Sir Matt Busby was still alive and there was a dinner after the match with the players and their wives and I spent the night just chatting to everybody. It was such a wonderful occasion because, for the first time, you could glimpse the potential of the team which has become such an awesome force. Yes – a fabulous night.

I looked up to Matt Busby so much, and still do, especially as he played for Manchester City! Personally, I always think it's great for the city to have two clubs challenging for honours. People like Brian Kidd and Denis Law who played for both clubs seem to bring the city together, which I enjoy, and which brings me to another point I wanted to make about the players you'll find in this book, and even those who haven't figured. And that is the debt they owe to the great managers, such as Sir Matt and Sir Alex, who have brought them to United and nurtured their talent. I'm sure Alex would say Sir Matt was better and vice versa, but one thing is for sure: that kind of management has a huge impact in keeping great players at the top of their game.

Mick Hucknall
June 2001

RALPH MILNE

Ralph Milne is the Eddie the Eagle of Manchester United ... so bad, but so popular, that he finds himself elected into the Greats!

Perhaps there is a guilt vote, too, because when he was at Old Trafford the fans gave him a hard time and he invariably figures when the fanzines nominate United's worst-ever team.

The fact that he was taking over the number 11 shirt from the entertaining Jesper Olsen didn't help him, but eventually I think there was a grudging admiration from the fans for the way the Scot tried to climb a mountain that got steeper every time he played.

Sir Alex Ferguson, who bought him from Bristol Rovers for £160,000 in November 1988, thought the Old Trafford stage was just too daunting for him and admits: "I came under fire over Ralph Milne. I signed him as short-term cover because I thought Gordon Strachan was leaving. I learned the hard way that as far as the United supporters are concerned, if you sign any 28-year-old player for a £160,000 fee, they regard him either as a cast-off or a dud. Stop-gaps just don't have a chance at Old Trafford."

PROFILE

BORN Dundee, Scotland
DATE OF BIRTH 13 May 1961
JOINED UNITED November 1988
FEE £160,000
PREVIOUS CLUBS Dundee United, Charlton Athletic, Bristol City
UNITED LEAGUE APPS 23
GOALS 3

"...when Joe Jordan said they had agreed a fee with another club, I was just stunned when he said it was Manchester United. I went to the manager's house to discuss terms but he could have offered me anything and I would have joined"

When Ralph's inclusion in the *Manchester United* magazine list of Greats was discussed at a press conference, someone wondered who had voted for him. A smiling Sir Alex loyally volunteered: "I did."

But there was nothing wrong with his pedigree. He played for Scotland at both youth and Under-21 levels. He signed professional forms for Dundee United at the age of 16 and made his debut at 18, coming on as a sub in a league game at Celtic. He scored the equaliser in a 2–2 draw. To top it off, he marked his full debut by scoring in a Scottish Cup tie against Dunfermline.

As he says himself: "We won the Premier Championship, and I played in four Cup finals during my time at Tannadice. Although we weren't one of the big three clubs, we still had success, even in Europe."

In fact, Milne scored 15 goals for Dundee United in five seasons of European football, a record to compare with the best. He joined Charlton Athletic for £125,000, but injuries cramped his style and he moved to Bristol City where things went so well that Manchester United came in for him.

Joe Jordan, the one-time United striker who was manager at Ashton Gate, called the player into his office. Says Milne: "I knew Aberdeen had been watching me so when Joe Jordan said they had agreed a fee with another club, I was just stunned when he said it was Manchester United. I went out to the manager's house to discuss terms but he could have offered me anything and I'd have joined."

The United management team of Alex Ferguson and Archie Knox were hardly strangers, but the Scot nevertheless found it difficult to settle at Old Trafford.

JOHN GIDMAN

John Gidman is another of the players who might be surprised to find himself voted into the top hundred Greats, albeit just squeezing in at number 99.

For like a few others, he flitted relatively briefly across the stage at Old Trafford without putting in the kind of service contributed by quite a few players who have been overlooked. The explanation of course is that while the fans might not have seen a lot of him, they liked what they saw, especially in the FA Cup run of 1984–85.

I am sure he won a lot of admirers that year with the way he had fought back after missing virtually two seasons with injury to become a key man on the run to Wembley. He came into the team at right-back for the fourth round and stayed there to help knock Liverpool out in the semi-final after a replay and then triumph 1–0 in the final against Everton.

Anyone who helps put one over both Merseyside clubs tends to be remembered anyway by United supporters, especially when you can produce the kind of attacking flair from full-back that was always the hallmark of Gidman's play.

Ron Atkinson was certainly one of the Liverpool-born player's admirers. He moved in quickly to make him his first signing following his arrival at Old Trafford to replace Dave Sexton in the summer of 1981. Atkinson gave Everton Mickey Thomas plus £450,000, and clearly considered he was striking a good deal, as he describes in his book: "Mickey Thomas came in to see me. From the moment he arrived in my office he just couldn't keep still. In fact, I became quite exhausted watching him constantly wriggling about in the chair. He asked me for a transfer and, when I sought a reason, he replied: 'Money, I just seem to spend more than I earn.' There was no answer to that.

"Fortunately, for me, I was aware that John Gidman was available for transfer. I had always liked the look of Gidman, having seen him in action on numerous occasions when he played for Aston Villa. Jimmy Nicholl was the established right-back at Manchester United but had never really impressed me. So when Thomas suggested his move, I had little hesitation in setting up a straight swap deal with Everton for Gidman."

Gidman, capped once for England after youth and Under-23 honours, settled in to play alongside Arthur Albiston in his first year, but then ran into two seasons of bad luck with a succession of injuries, which included nearly being blinded in one eye by a firework.

He had to watch Mike Duxbury take his position but he never lost either hope or confidence and returned to squeeze his rival into a midfield role and play with style in the successful FA Cup season. The following year was a ding-dong battle with Duxbury for the right-back position until he had to acknowledge defeat and accept a free transfer in October 1986, to join Manchester City. After two years at Maine Road, he moved to Stoke City, and had a short spell at Darlington as assistant manager before becoming manager of King's Lynn.

Mick Brown, United's coach under Ron Atkinson and now chief scout at Old Trafford, recalls: "John was one of the first out-and-out attacking full-backs. He was very talented and should have won more than one full cap for England. A very bubbly character, his nickname of 'Giddy' was appropriate."

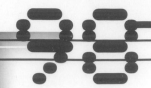

MARK ROBINS

Sir Alex Ferguson knows better than anyone why Mark Robins figures among the Greats of Manchester United.

For though the Oldham youngster failed to become a regular in the first team at Old Trafford, he has a secure place in the affections of the United manager, and fans realise that but for Robins, the Ferguson success story might never have happened.

Season 1989–90 found Sir Alex at crisis point. He had spent a lot of money in the close season bringing in players like Gary Pallister, Paul Ince and Danny Wallace, but there had been no noticeable improvement on the previous season's finishing position of 11th. His team were drifting steadily downwards and by January the knives were out.

The FA Cup had suddenly taken on a crucial importance and when the third round produced a draw taking United to Nottingham Forest, the prospects looked ominous.

Enter Mark Robins, the saviour in Alex Ferguson's hour of need. United had been hit by injuries and Robins had only started in two League games that season before the cup tie, but he rose to the occasion and scored for a 1–0 win which confounded all the critics.

It was a golden goal which launched United on to a run which took them all the way to Wembley and a replay victory over Crystal Palace which gave Ferguson his first trophy with United

PROFILE

BORN Ashton-under-Lyne, Manchester
DATE OF BIRTH 22 December 1968
JOINED UNITED July 1986
FEE None
PREVIOUS CLUB Junior
UNITED LEAGUE APPS 48
GOALS 11

and was the ice-breaker which brought him time to see him become Manchester United's most successful manager since Sir Matt Busby.

Ferguson will certainly never forget the Forest match.

He recalls: "Everybody was smelling defeat for us. Jimmy Hill even said we looked like a beaten team in the warm-up. We were without regulars like Webb, Robson and Ince, but the lads I picked performed magnificently. They worked themselves into the ground and got a deserved 1–0 win with a goal scored by Mark Robins, bless him. It was a happy dressing room and you could sense the players and directors were happy for me after all the speculation about my future following our rough ride in the League."

Robins, who had joined United from junior football in Oldham and the Lilleshall School of Excellence, continued to shoot the team to Wembley. He scored at Newcastle in the fifth round and then got the all-important winner against Oldham Athletic in a semi-final replay.

He came on as a substitute in the 3–3 draw against Crystal Palace at Wembley, but there was no place for him in the starting line-up for the replay which United won 1–0.

Although he was a natural and predatory goal scorer with international honours at youth and Under-21 levels, he never commanded a regular first-team place and after asking for a transfer in 1992, he joined Norwich for £800,000.

Mark also played for Leicester City, FC Copenhagen, Reading, Ourense in Spain, Panionios in Greece, Manchester City briefly on loan, Walsall and Rotherham, where he continued to score with the ease associated with him throughout his well-travelled career.

> "Jimmy Hill said we looked like a beaten team in the warm-up. They worked themselves into the ground and got a deserved 1-0 win with a goal scored by Mark Robins, bless him."
>
> SIR ALEX FERGUSON

LUKE CHADWICK

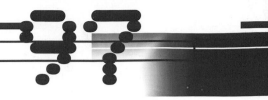

Luke Chadwick is the new kid on the block, and appearing here among the Greats more for his rich potential than for what he has achieved so far.

We should be amazed that he is voted into the list at all because he is only just starting out. Obviously he has already impressed the readers of the *Manchester United* magazine, so exciting is he to watch.

As Sir Alex Ferguson says: "Luke has a special talent which is emerging more dramatically now that he is getting stronger. He gives me a good option on the right wing with his ability to dribble and go past defenders."

It is, of course, this tremendous capacity to jink past opponents which catches the imagination. Even in those last sad and despairing minutes in last season's quarter-final defeat against Bayern Munich in the European Champions League the youngster lit up Old Trafford with the way he mesmerised the German defence after coming on as a late substitute.

He almost scored, or at least laid on a goal as he cut in from the right wing, and he made it look so easy. You wondered what might have happened had he come on earlier; perhaps that's wishful thinking, but there is no doubt that he is going to figure among the Greats of the future as an achiever rather than simply for what he promises!

That may come sooner than we think: he was given an extended run in the first team at the end of last season, after the Premiership had been tied up, with the manager taking the opportunity to test him at the highest level.

He was still only 20 when Sir Alex registered him for the Champions League just before last Christmas, reflecting the speed of his progress after he was sent for a season to Royal Antwerp, United's feeder club in Belgium, where he helped the First Division club win promotion in 2000.

Brought up in Cambridge, he went to Arsenal's school of excellence and was offered terms by both United and Highbury.

"I thought that Old Trafford was much friendlier so I came north," he says. "Playing in Belgium toughened me mentally and physically because first-team football does not allow you to make mistakes.

"Last season United gave me a four-year contract, which was the best moment of my life."

England have naturally picked up on him, and after playing for the Under-18s he became a regular in the Under-21 side, scoring on his debut in a 5–0 win against Luxembourg.

Although he didn't come back to Old Trafford until October of last season, he still managed to make 22 appearances in the first team, 16 of those in the Premiership, which easily qualified him for a Championship medal.

His emergence as a winger capable of playing on either flank gives the manager the option of moving David Beckham to a midfield role.

As Luke Chadwick says: "There might be something there for me if that ever happens. David Beckham is the best in the world in his position and being able to learn from him and the rest of the United players is good enough for me at the moment."

His style inevitably reminds you of George Best, who says: "The thing I like about him is that he likes to take-players on. I love to see that."

PROFILE

BORN Cambridge
DATE OF BIRTH 18 November 1980
JOINED UNITED June 1997
FEE None
PREVIOUS CLUB Junior
UNITED LEAGUE APPS 16
GOALS 2

"The thing I like about him is that he likes to take players on."

GEORGE BEST

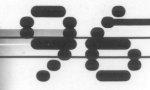

MIKE DUXBURY

The mastery of the English language shown by our footballers from overseas, especially the Norwegians, Dutch and Danes, never ceases to impress me, and we perhaps forget at times that they, in turn, have to understand us.

I believe, for instance, that it can take a week or two before some of the foreign players at Old Trafford are able to comprehend every facet of the Scottish brogue of their manager.

Quite what they would have made of that splendid voice from the Rossendale Valley which belonged to Mike Duxbury 20 years ago, I don't know. It was a rich and pure echo from Lancashire which travelling the world as a footballer did little to soften. Nor should it have done, because there was something particularly sturdy and dependable about his accent that exactly reflected his quality as a player.

He continued to live at Rossendale after joining United as a youngster in 1976 and, away from the game, he had his lurcher dog, his ferrets and a love for the countryside and eventually, of course, his family.

He worked his way up through the junior teams and reserves and once he had broken into the first team enjoyed 10 years at the top, appearing in nearly 400 games. As you might expect from such an able and willing team member, he was versatile, and played in a number of positions ranging from midfield to defence.

Like others before him, his career might have suffered a little from being moved around so often. As he once explained to me: "When I first came into the team and was picked in different positions it was good, because it helped you to learn about the game. As time goes by you want to settle in one spot. I did that at right-back for a long time, but then I was moved around again and things went downhill for a time."

His fortunes revived when he was selected at left-back by Alex Ferguson, which rather surprised him.

"Never in a million years did I expect to find myself at left-back. It came out of the blue, and to be honest I found it embarrassing, because Arthur Albiston played there and I felt awkward with him after what he had done for the club. Of course at the end of the day we are all professionals and you play where you are picked."

It was Dave Sexton who gave him his full senior debut against Manchester City at Old Trafford and said about him: "Young Mike came through to show himself not only extremely versatile but a performer of assurance. I can turn to him with as much confidence as anyone else."

He had to prove himself all over again when Ron Atkinson arrived and immediately signed John Gidman for right-back, but he fought back and eventually settled at right-back in a long-term partnership with Arthur Albiston. They had nearly three seasons together in Duxbury's most successful period at the club.

Already an England Under-21 international with a European Championship medal after beating Germany in the final, he was picked for the full England side and won 10 caps. With his club he played in the FA Cup-winning teams of 1983 and 1985 before working for his third manager.

He impressed Alex Ferguson and played for him for three seasons before moving nearer home to Blackburn Rovers. He had a spell with Bradford City and also played in Hong Kong where he had the unusual experience of playing against England, who were on a flag-flying tour. More recently he has worked in Bolton as a PE teacher.

PROFILE

BORN Accrington
DATE OF BIRTH 1 September 1959
JOINED UNITED July 1976
FEE None
PREVIOUS CLUB Junior
UNITED LEAGUE APPS 299
GOALS 6
INTERNATIONAL CAPS (England) 10
GOALS 0

"Young Mike came through to show himself not only extremely versatile but a player of assurance."

DAVE SEXTON

LES SEALEY

You probably won't find the name of Les Sealey cropping up too much in any discussion about Manchester United's all-time great goalkeepers, but in terms of popularity he most certainly deserves to be included among the Greats, as well as for the way he answered emergency calls with distinction.

PROFILE

BORN Bethnal Green, London
DATE OF BIRTH 29 September 1957
JOINED UNITED June 1990, also 1993
FEE £30,000
PREVIOUS CLUBS Coventry City, Luton Town
UNITED LEAGUE APPS 33
GOALS 0

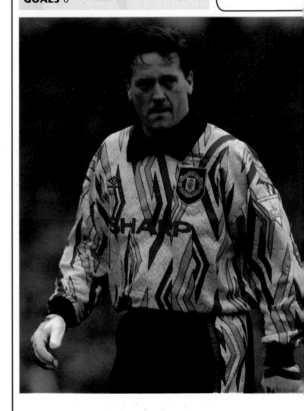

He made only 55 first-team appearances after initially coming to Old Trafford on loan from Luton in 1989, and he used to tell me he felt every day he spent with Manchester United was like Christmas Day, except this was a fairy story come true. His whole approach reflected his enthusiasm and the joy he always found in playing football in a well-travelled career.

But though he played for fun he was deadly serious about his performances, and when Sealey was dramatically selected to replace Jim Leighton for the FA Cup final replay against Crystal Palace in 1990 it was certainly no laughing matter.

Leighton, who had wobbled in the drawn game, was distraught at being dropped – a reaction which added to the pressure on Sealey as he stepped out at Wembley for his first appearance in the FA Cup for United, and after only two League games.

It's not easy keeping goal for Manchester United – just ask Mark Bosnich and Massimo Taibi – but Sealey, ever the cheeky Londoner, was a rock of confidence as United won the replay 1–0 through Lee Martin's rare goal.

As Sir Alex Ferguson describes it, "Leighton's misfortune was Les Sealey's big break. He's not daft and knew what was expected of him. His confident, almost cocky, approach ensured that he not only enjoyed Wembley, but did a good job. Right from the start he made a good save and handled the ball with the kind of assurance that injects confidence into the whole defence. After he helped us clinch the Cup it was only fair that I should offer him a one-year contract, which he accepted."

The extended stay enabled Sealey to produce more heroics for United, and he certainly won admirers when he played in the final of the Rumbelows Cup against Sheffield Wednesday in place of the suspended Peter Schmeichel. He was hurt in a goal-mouth collision which left his knee gashed right down to the bone. Physiotherapist Jim McGregor wanted him to come off, but Sealey was so determined to stay on that at one point it looked as if he was going to hit the United medical man unless he stopped trying to take him out of the game.

I suppose when your chances are few and far between you don't let go easily, so he stayed to finish the game and persuaded the manager he was fit enough to play in the final of the European Cup Winners' Cup against Barcelona in Rotterdam a few days later.

He finished the game limping, and though he was beaten by Ronald Koeman's free kick he dug in to see United through to the 2–1 win which was so important for Sir Alex Ferguson's career at that point.

After a job well done he was soon on the move again and played for Aston Villa, and Coventry again, before another loan period at United as cover for Schmeichel in 1993.

There were no big-time emergencies

> "After he helped us clinch the Cup it was only fair that I should offer him a one-year contract."
>
> SIR ALEX FERGUSON

this time, though, and he soon resumed his travels to appear at Blackpool and West Ham.

CLAYTON BLACKMORE

Clayton Blackmore made it into the list of Greats, but with the talent he was blessed with, he perhaps should have appeared a lot higher in the list than this. I suspect the popular and likeable Welshman didn't always drive himself as hard as he might have done.

H e was a lovely player, strong, skilful and stylish, but United's fanzine didn't nickname him "Sunbed" for nothing, maybe feeling that what seemed to be an all-year suntan reflected his laid-back approach to life and football.

Perhaps his initial success came too easily. He was a Welsh international from schoolboy level all the way through to youth, Under-21 and senior levels, and was capped for Wales at junior level 17 times, an achievement which even bettered that of his contemporary Mark Hughes.

"Mark and I have been mates for a few years now after first meeting when we were having trials for the Welsh schoolboy team," he says.

"He was already at United, while I had just joined, and so he brought me a United tracksuit to wear at the trials. We've been pals ever since."

The friendship has lasted to the present day with Mark, as manager of Wales, appointing Clayton to run his Under-15 team, with some success.

United had Clayton on their books as an associated schoolboy from the age of 14, and he made his first-team debut in 1984 for Ron Atkinson when

he was still only 19. Somehow, though, his ascent began to slow and he found it hard to establish himself as a regular in the Old Trafford team. One problem might have been that he was too versatile, never concentrating on one position; at various times he wore every shirt number except the goalkeeper's.

With Wales, it was never a problem. He was playing for his country at senior level after only two first-team appearances for his club. At United he was an ever-ready reserve, but not until two or three years after his debut could he claim a position right through a season.

His athleticism appealed to Sir Alex Ferguson and he gave him more opportunities, mostly at left-back. He bagged a winner's medal for a substitute appearance in the 1990 FA Cup final against Crystal Palace, but the following year was his most successful.

He played at Wembley in the League Cup final against Sheffield Wednesday and then two months later in the team which beat Barcelona in Rotterdam to win the European Cup Winners' Cup.

He had a particularly glorious moment late in the game, described by his manager thus: "The biggest heart-stopping moment came when Clayton Blackmore kicked off the line. There were only three minutes to go and everyone who saw it will remember Clayton for ever. Laudrup side-footed the ball towards an empty net and Clayton had read it brilliantly."

The glory was short-lived. Clayton found it increasingly difficult to get into the team and in 1994 was given a free transfer which saw him snapped up by former team-mate Bryan Robson at Middlesbrough. After five years at the Riverside Stadium, he then played for Barnsley and Notts County. Still playing non-League football, he was last spotted playing for Bangor.

PROFILE

BORN Neath, Wales
DATE OF BIRTH 23 September 1964
JOINED UNITED June 1981
FEE None
PREVIOUS CLUB Junior
UNITED LEAGUE APPS 186
GOALS 19
INTERNATIONAL CAPS (Wales) 39
GOALS 1

"Everyone who saw Clayton kick off the line will remember it for ever."
SIR ALEX FERGUSON ON CLAYTON BLACKMORE'S 1991 EUROPEAN CUP WINNERS' CUP FINAL GLORY

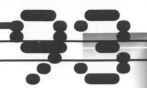

MIKAEL SILVESTRE

Mikael Silvestre has been fortunate: he has a manager who not only had tremendous faith in him but also never lost it through what was undoubtedly a rough passage.

The Frenchman did not have the best of starts to his career at Old Trafford following his £4-million transfer from Inter Milan in September 1999.

He obviously had talent but also had a habit of making costly mistakes, and the fans certainly lacked confidence in him. Sir Alex Ferguson never wavered, though, and explained, "Mikael might make mistakes and I have no doubt that I could play someone else and he would probably do better for us. But I am looking ahead and Mikael has one priceless asset, which is his pace. You can rarely put speed into a player, so it is worth cultivating, and when he has completed his learning curve the boy will be an exceptionally good player."

And that's exactly how it has worked out, with Silvestre now so good and such a favourite with the supporters that he has gatecrashed the list of United Greats!

Although he arrived expressing a preference for centre-back and had a good run alongside Jaap Stam in season 1999–2000, he needed the support of the manager to hold his place.

Last season, though, he came into his own, and with a switch of position to left-back played in 46 competitive games. Only Gary Neville appeared in more, which tells the story of the young defender's dramatic recovery. The fans last season took to him in a big way, especially when he made one of his typical lightning-quick runs forward.

Although two seasons have seen him score only one goal – albeit a cracker against Leicester at Old Trafford, after replacing Phil Neville – he looks destined to score a lot more.

His form last season did not go unnoticed in France and he was called up to the senior squad for a series of friendlies before making his full debut in a four-goal win against Portugal. Winning a place in the World Cup holders' team could not have been easy but Silvestre seems to be well-established now. As his fellow-international, Fabien Barthez, says: "At his age very few defenders have such a good reputation. He has a strong potential and rarely loses the ball."

The player himself appreciates the fact that the Old Trafford crowd now accepts him.

"I was aware of the criticism. You can't ignore it, but you do get used to it. At Inter Milan, I had my car vandalised by fans," he said.

His acceptance is important to him because he believes team spirit is an essential part of United's success, as he explained: "To my mind, the reason why Arsenal haven't been able to keep pace with us is that they don't have enough English players. We are far more in tune with the Premiership. The pillars of the squad have grown up together and the players brought in have fitted into the mould."

Early in his career, when he was transferred to Inter Milan from Rennes, he had mixed fortunes and became unsettled.

"When I was told about United's offer I answered, 'Yes' immediately," says Silvestre.

"After what I went through in Italy, I knew I was ready to cope with a new adventure."

Some adventure, too, with two Championship medals to his name in two years and now one of the family!

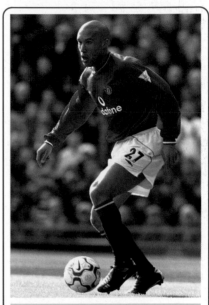

PROFILE

BORN Chambray-les-Tours, France
DATE OF BIRTH 9 August 1977
JOINED UNITED September 1999
FEE £4 million
PREVIOUS CLUBS Rennes, Inter Milan
UNITED LEAGUE APPS 61
GOALS 1
INTERNATIONAL CAPS 4
GOALS 1

"At his age very few defenders have such a good reputation. He has a strong potential and rarely loses the ball."
FABIEN BARTHEZ

JESPER BLOMQVIST

Jesper Blomqvist must rate as currently the unluckiest player at Old Trafford.

Injury has savaged his career, and the fact that you find his name in this top 100 at all speaks volumes for the way the fans admired his skills when he was first signed from Parma by Sir Alex Ferguson in the summer of 1998.

Even then we had to wait a month to see him in action because he arrived from Italy with a foot injury. Once he got going, though, making his debut in a 4–1 win over Charlton at Old Trafford, he was a very capable deputy on the left wing for Ryan Giggs. In fact, the manager said that if United had had the Swedish international as cover for Giggs the previous year, he felt they would have won the Championship instead of finishing a point behind Arsenal, and might well have got past Monaco in the Champions' League.

Of course Ferguson had been a long-time admirer of Blomqvist, remembering only too painfully how he had tormented United in a European Champions League match when he played for Gothenberg. Recently voted Sweden's Player of the Year, he sparkled in a 3–1 win for his Swedish club which just about put paid to United's hopes of qualifying for the knock-out stage of the 1994 competition.

United would have liked to have bought him then, but he went instead to play for AC Milan and then Parma. When he became available in Italy, Ferguson moved in with a £4.4-million fee and found him a useful addition to the squad as they set about the marathon task of winning the treble.

The manager left him out of the FA Cup final but played him four days later in the Champions League final as he juggled his squad to maximum effect.

"I took the precaution of leaving Jesper out against Newcastle at Wembley because at the time I intended to play Ryan Giggs in midfield against Bayern with Jesper on the wing," he explained. "I told him before the Cup final game because I knew it would buck him up after his initial disappointment."

In all, Jesper made 38 appearances in the treble season, little suspecting that his game against Bayern Munich in Barcelona would be his last competitive fixture for two years. Thrilled by his European medal, he had great hopes for the following season but injured his knee on the pre-season tour.

He barely recovered his fitness in time for the next pre-season warm-up, only to damage his other knee. A succession of operations wiped out an entire season for the second year running. A lot of his time was spent back home in Sweden as he fought – and is still fighting – for his football future.

It is all a far cry from his early career and the realisation of a dream to play in English football.

"It was hard for me in Milan," he said. "The team were not playing well and as a new player it was difficult for me to settle. I enjoyed it more at Parma, where I became a better defensive player as well as playing as an attacking winger. But I think I am going to enjoy it more in the Premiership. The football in England is more fun than in Italy."

Some fun! Little did he know what lay ahead, though playing in a winning team in the final of the European Champions League must be a modicum of consolation!

Now out of contract, he has asked to stay on without pay to train with the Reds pre-season in a bid for fitness.

PROFILE

BORN Tavelsjo, Sweden
DATE OF BIRTH 5 February 1974
JOINED UNITED August 1998
FEE £4.4 million
PREVIOUS CLUBS Umea, Gothenberg, AC Milan, Parma
UNITED LEAGUE APPS 25
GOALS 1
INTERNATIONAL CAPS (Sweden) 29
GOALS 0

"I think I am going to enjoy it more in the Premiership. The football in England is more fun than in Italy."

JESPER BLOMQVIST

WILF McGUINNESS

Brian Clough once called Wilf McGuinness "a sacrificial lamb".

The controversial Clough was having a dig at Manchester United by suggesting that they had not given him a chance when they made him the manager in succession to Sir Matt Busby in 1969.

It's true, of course, that Wilf was given only 18 months before they sacked him, and the appointment was certainly akin to a poisoned chalice. How on earth they expected such a young man to sort out the ageing 1968 European glory team is anyone's guess, but I am sure Sir Matt and the board had the best of intentions.

The irony is that in his short time at the helm his team twice finished eighth in the First Division and reached three Cup semi-finals – not exactly a story of failure – and it was never going to be easy dealing with the big stars like Bobby Charlton, Pat Crerand, Denis Law and Alex Stepney, who were all coming to the end of their careers.

It was a stressful time all round and Wilf certainly felt it. His hair turned white and eventually dropped out as he licked his wounds abroad as the manager of Aris Salonika in Greece. He came home to manage York City and took them through a couple of divisions, unfortunately only going down! He worked briefly in Hull before studying physiotherapy and joining the staff at Bury.

His rough ride as a manager at Old Trafford may have picked up a sympathy vote to ease him into the Greats list, but he is also there in his own right as a player. A broken leg at the age of 22 ended his playing career, otherwise I am sure he would have gone right to the top for both club and country. As it was, he had a superb pedigree as a schoolboy captain all the way up to international level, where one of the players under his command was none

other than his friend Bobby Charlton – something he was not slow to remind us all about as Bobby became a legend.

Wilf had already won two full England caps himself when injury struck, a blow which did nothing to reduce his vigour and enthusiasm for the game. These were the qualities which first prompted Sir Matt to bring him on to the club's coaching staff and then pick him out as part of the United family to become his successor. Alf Ramsey also had Wilf in his coaching team for the 1966 World Cup.

It was circumstance rather than any lack of ability which saw the United appointment fail, and in my view he more than deserves to be in the hall of fame for what he achieved in his short time as a player, as well as the way he then refused to allow disappointment to suck him into a slough of bitterness.

It meant he was cheerfully able to maintain his close connections with United. He is the match analyser on the club radio, a host in their hospitality suites and a superb master of ceremonies at many club functions, as well as being a hugely popular success on the after-dinner speaking circuit.

PROFILE

BORN Manchester
DATE OF BIRTH 25 October 1937
JOINED UNITED January 1953
FEE None
PREVIOUS CLUB Junior
UNITED LEAGUE APPS 81
GOALS 2
INTERNATIONAL CAPS (England) 2
GOALS 0

"His rough ride as a manager may have picked up a sympathy vote to ease him into the Greats list, but he is also there in his own right as a player."

IAN STOREY-MOORE

Ian Storey-Moore made a mere 39 League appearances for Manchester United and it is a testimony to his dramatic wing play and the entertainment value of the 11 goals he scored that he has made the top hundred Greats after such a meagre contribution.

In fact, Ian himself looks back with mixed feelings on his career at Old Trafford, having been signed by Frank O'Farrell in March 1972 shortly after the team's slide down the table began.

United had held a five-point lead at the top of the table at Christmas and O'Farrell paid Nottingham Forest £200,000 in an attempt to steady a rocking boat.

It was no fault of the player, but the spiral was out of control and Storey-Moore says: "It was a terrible time to be with the club. It was a transitional period; the older players resented the newer ones, there were a lot of cliques and it wasn't a friendly atmosphere, which was probably reflected in our performances out on the field.

"Manchester United are a great club, of course, and I was happy to join them. I was just disappointed that I was not there for the good times. I hit the club at the wrong period, and then wrecked my ankle so badly that I hard-ly played for Tommy Docherty after Frank O'Farrell had been sacked.

"I had to finish with League football at the age of 27. I returned to the Nottingham area where I had business interests. I went into non-League football and twice took Burton Albion through to the first round proper of the FA Cup as player-manager.

"Bill Foulkes took me out to America to play for Chicago Sting for a while, but my ankle went again. I was manager of Shepshed Charterhouse for two or three years. I had a newsagent's for 18 months, but mostly I have been involved in my betting offices and bookmaking. I left football behind me but I did enjoy a return to Old Trafford some time ago when television invited me to cover a game against Nottingham Forest."

Ian made his name playing at Forest, of course, and enjoyed some good times at that stage. His most successful season came in 1966–67 when Johnny Carey took them to second place in the Championship behind Manchester United and to the FA Cup semi-finals.

"I remember that season vividly. We beat United on our ground but lost 1–0 at Old Trafford thanks to Denis Law scoring with a spectacular overhead bicycle kick," he recalled.

But once O'Farrell had signed him, things began to go wrong. Even the transfer was far from smooth. After initially failing to agree terms with United, Brian Clough moved in and actually paraded him round the Baseball Ground as Derby County's new signing. The forms didn't have a signature from Forest, though, and United were able to complete the transfer the following week.

Ian must wonder if he would have had better luck if Brian Clough had succeeded with his smash-and-grab raid!

PROFILE

BORN Ipswich
DATE OF BIRTH 17 January 1945
JOINED UNITED March 1972
FEE £200,000
PREVIOUS CLUB Nottingham Forest
UNITED LEAGUE APPS 39
GOALS 11
INTERNATIONAL CAPS (England) 1
GOALS 0

> "Manchester United are a great club and I was happy to join them. I was just disappointed that I was not there for the good times."
>
> IAN STOREY-MOORE LOOKS BACK ON HIS
> ALL-TOO-BRIEF CAREER AT OLD TRAFFORD

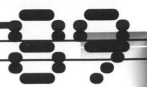

HENRY COCKBURN

As one-time Busby Babe John Doherty put it: "Henry Cockburn played left-half off his right foot for 10 seasons and he was magnificent."

"He was nothing in weight or size, but he was an early-day Nobby Stiles. His throw-ins were a joke, but he shouted and he kicked a bit. He was as honest as the day was long and it was lovely to play in the same team with him. He was particularly great for the kids starting to come into the team," said Doherty.

And that, of course, was a bonus for Manchester United, because not only was Henry a key element in Matt Busby's first post-war team, but he played on into the era which saw the first of the Busby Babes – like John Doherty – making their way into the first team. He was one of the players who gave the club continuity as the manager broke up the old guard in order to introduce his home-developed youngsters.

An Ashton-under-Lyne boy, he joined United from their nursery club, Goslings, and made his first-team debut in wartime football. So he was nicely ready to join the team which won the FA Cup in 1948 and the Championship four years later.

Charlie Mitten certainly enjoyed the early days playing in front of him on the left wing, and recalled not so long ago for Ivan Ponting: "He was right-footed but fitted in well on the left. When Henry got the ball I always knew I would be the next to touch it. There wasn't much of him; he was very light; but when he made a tackle his opponent knew all about it. He played an important part in what we achieved."

He stayed in the side to help develop the next great team until even the mighty Cockburn was forced to concede his place to the challenge of a new generation of players like Jeff Whitefoot and Duncan Edwards. By then the former mill-fitter had played nearly 300 games for United and become a favourite with the crowd, not least for the way he could outjump much taller opponents despite his lack of height.

His quality was quickly recognised by England and he was capped after relatively few League games to win a total of 13 caps and forge a formidable half-back line with Stoke City's Neil Franklin at centre-half and Billy Wright, the captain of Wolves, at right-half. It was rated one of the best international half-back lines of all time.

He left United in 1954 to play for Bury and then Peterborough before other non-League stints with teams like Corby and Sankeys. There was no bowing out at the top for Henry Cockburn; he loved playing so much that he was happy to slide down the leagues.

He also coached, and was a trainer with Oldham and Huddersfield before retiring from the game, but continued to live locally and keep in touch with United and his many friends through the Former Players' Association.

PROFILE

BORN Ashton-under-Lyne, Manchester
DATE OF BIRTH 14 September 1923
JOINED UNITED September 1943
FEE None
PREVIOUS CLUB Goslings
UNITED LEAGUE APPS 243
GOALS 4
INTERNATIONAL CAPS (England) 13
GOALS 0

"His throw-ins were a joke, but he shouted and he kicked a bit. He was as honest as the day was long and it was lovely to play in the same team with him. He was particularly great for the kids starting to come into the team."
BUSBY BABE JOHN DOHERTY

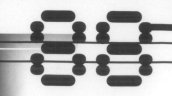

FRANK STAPLETON

Manchester United could have had Frank Stapleton as a young teenager if they had wished and also, for good measure, another Irish youngster destined for great things – David O'Leary.

Billy Behan, United's ace scout in Dublin for 50 rewarding years, sent both boys over for trials at Old Trafford in 1971 when they were 15, but Frank O'Farrell had more pressing first-team problems on his mind and his staff didn't see anything particularly promising about the two shy youngsters.

Arsenal did, though, and quickly signed both of them up as apprentices at Highbury, with the result that 10 years later it cost United £900,000 to bring Stapleton to Old Trafford. O'Leary didn't do badly for the Gunners either!

But even at nearly a million pounds Stapleton was excellent value, and a good piece of business, because the player was out of contract at Highbury and the fee was settled by an independent tribunal. Arsenal had valued him at £1.5 million and were exceedingly piqued at being forced to accept what they considered a cut-price fee.

Ron Atkinson, who reckoned the player was another Tommy Taylor with similar qualities as a bustling centre-forward, was naturally delighted and said: "Frank's style of play reminds me very much of Taylor; powerful in the air and good on the ground.

"I was delighted to get my man. He not only replaced Joe Jordan, who had gone to Italy, as a centre-forward and goal-scorer, but he also captured the hearts of a public who had been good fans of Big Joe.

"We certainly had no complaints about the deal. Frank proved to be exceedingly good value for the money, even if Arsenal did take umbrage at losing such a prized player for £900,000. At least we paid the fee all in one lump sum, a rare occurrence in modern-day football."

Arsenal had every right to feel sore at losing a player who had scored 108 goals for them from 299 appearances and helped them win the FA Cup in 1979 by scoring in a 3–2 win over Manchester United.

Four years later Frank would open the scoring for United at Wembley against Brighton to become the first player to score an FA Cup final goal with two different clubs.

He collected another FA Cup winners' medal with United in 1985 as a member of the side which beat Everton.

In all he made nearly 300 appearances for United and scored 78 goals. He played under Alex Ferguson but not for long. He never really hit it off with the new manager, and with Brian McClair on his way to Old Trafford he was transferred to Ajax at the end of Ferguson's first season.

Strangely, he made only four appearances for the Dutch club before a loan period with Derby County and then spells with French club Le Havre and Blackburn Rovers.

On the international front he had a distinguished career with the Republic of Ireland, captaining his country, winning 70 caps and scoring a record 20 goals.

Married to a Manchester girl, he lives in Bowdon, Cheshire, and maintains links with Manchester United as a broadcaster with local and national radio stations as well as appearing on Manchester United TV.

PROFILE

BORN Dublin
DATE OF BIRTH 10 July 1956
JOINED UNITED August 1981
FEE £900,000
PREVIOUS CLUB Arsenal
UNITED LEAGUE APPS 223
GOALS 60
INTERNATIONAL CAPS (Republic of Ireland) 70
GOALS 20

"We certainly had no complaints about the deal. Frank proved to be exceedingly good value for the money, even if Arsenal did take umbrage at losing such a prized player for £900,000."

RON ATKINSON ON FRANK STAPLETON'S ARRIVAL

LEE MARTIN

Who among Manchester United supporters can forget the goal that won the FA Cup at Wembley in 1990 to take the pressure off Sir Alex Ferguson?

The Reds' manager was under fire with his team in the bottom half of the table, and it was a key victory that bought him time.

It was a golden goal never to be forgotten, certainly not by the Greats' voters and definitely not by the scorer himself!

"How could I forget that goal?" says Lee Martin, the full-back who burst forward to hammer a 1–0 replay-winner into the roof of the Crystal Palace net. "After all, I scored only one other for the first team in my 10 years at Old Trafford, and that was a fluke against West Ham when Alvin Martin kicked the ball against my legs and it went back past him into his own net.

"People often mention my Wembley goal but I never get fed up with hearing about it because it was the highlight of my career. I just remember Archie Knox, our coach, shouting from the bench for me to get forward and so I made a run. Neil Webb picked me out perfectly and I just whacked it. To be honest, it could have gone anywhere – and they usually did when I got near goal – but this one just flew in.

"People tell me now how important that goal was for Sir Alex Ferguson, like the one Mark Robins scored at Forest to see us through the third round, but as a young lad of 20 I wasn't aware of all the talk.

"I know we finished about 16th in the League but it never entered my head at the time that there was any possibility of the manager getting the sack. You had enough on your plate just coping with the pressure of needing to do well yourself without thinking too much about the Boss's position.

"I had been a regular all season and I played most of the following season. After that, though, I struggled to hold my place and by 1994 I was on a monthly contract when out of the blue I had a call from Lou Macari asking me if I was interested in going to play for him at Glasgow Celtic.

"Carl Muggleton from Stoke City was the only other Englishman there but the Scots made me feel very welcome and I enjoyed my two and a half years at Celtic Park.

"Unfortunately I had a bad time with injuries. I broke my leg, then my arm and finally I got two slipped discs," he says.

"It just got worse and worse. I could hardly run and I had to have an operation on my back.

"I finished there in May of 1998 and still get pain with my back."

Lee Martin is back living at Glossop, close to Hyde where he grew up, and Sir Alex Ferguson certainly demonstrated he had not forgotten his Wembley goal when, immediately after achieving the treble, he sent a testimonial team to play at Bristol Rovers to help a player who didn't score often, but when he did – it counted!

PROFILE

BORN Hyde, Manchester
DATE OF BIRTH 5 February 1968
JOINED UNITED June 1985
FEE None
PREVIOUS CLUB Junior
UNITED LEAGUE APPS 73
GOALS 1
INTERNATIONAL CAPS (England) 0

"People often talk about my Wembley goal but I never get tired of hearing about it."
LEE MARTIN RECALLS THE BEST MOMENT IN HIS CAREER

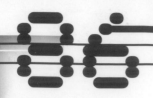

ALBERT QUIXALL

PROFILE

BORN Sheffield
DATE OF BIRTH 9 August 1933
JOINED UNITED September 1958
FEE £45,000
PREVIOUS CLUB
Sheffield Wednesday
UNITED LEAGUE APPS 165
GOALS 50
INTERNATIONAL CAPS (England) 5
GOALS 0

"Albert's contribution was an important one. He maintained the tradition of creative, attacking football and brought charisma to the club at a time of great crisis to help bridge the gap left by the Munich tragedy."

In his era, just after the Munich air crash, Albert Quixall was the golden boy of football.

In his native Sheffield he had swept everything before him: captain of his school, his city, his county, his country and playing for the full England team by the time he was 18.

He had played 243 League games for his local club, Sheffield Wednesday, scoring 63 goals, when Matt Busby paid them a then-record £45,000 for him a few months after the Munich accident. Busby was striving to rebuild the club with an emphasis on entertainment and personality, as well as basic prowess, because this had become part of the tradition at Old Trafford and Albert Quixall had delightful skills.

It wasn't a highly-successful period for United, of course, more a matter of keeping heads above water, and it was therefore difficult for an individual to shine as brightly as some of the later stars who played for United.

But Albert's contribution was an important one. He maintained the tradition of creative, attacking football and brought charisma to the club at a time of great crisis to help bridge the gap left by the Munich tragedy. Bill Foulkes said that the football played by the attacking trio of Quixall, Viollet and Charlton was as good as any he had seen.

He was well aware of the crash because he was skipper of the Sheffield Wednesday team which met United at Old Trafford in their first game after Munich, in the fifth round of the FA Cup. Albert always said it was an impossible game for them, with the whole country willing the survivors to win.

Fresh-faced and always youthful-looking with his mop of blond hair, he had a broad Yorkshire accent, an easy-going and friendly nature and was married to a former ballet dancer. There was nothing demanding about him, which may be why he chose to join United rather then take up an offer to go to London with Arsenal and earn a lot more.

He played in the days of the maximum wage and explained to me one day: "I suppose I was born 20 years too early in terms of money. I remember an article about me at the time of my transfer saying my record fee made me literally worth my weight in gold. It didn't make me a personal fortune, though I don't harp on it because you can't translate everything into money. I achieved a lot in my teens and had some great times in football. I'm not bitter by any means."

Certainly he missed the gravy train caught just a few years later by the stars following him. The result was a much more modest lifestyle after his United career and his one honour, the 1963 FA Cup. He joined Oldham for £8,500 in 1964 and also played for Stockport. He then ran a scrap-metal business in Manchester with one of his sons for his friend, Freddie Pye. It was a business he was introduced to by Fred at the time players were threatening to strike for the abolition of the maximum wage.

Never a man for pretensions, after his United days Albert combined the scrapyard with playing non-League football for Altrincham, the team managed by his benefactor. After struggling against an illness at one point in his life, he never went back across the Pennines, and made Manchester his adopted home.

JESPER OLSEN

You could understand Ron Atkinson's enthusiasm when he signed Jesper Olsen for £500,000.

A slightly built but tantalisingly elusive winger with all manner of tricks, the diminutive Dane shot to prominence when he joined Ajax and was in the talented team which twice won the Dutch Championship and enjoyed a Cup success.

He also put his skills to work for the Danish national team, winning 43 caps and scoring a particularly impressive goal against England in the European Championship of 1982.

At Old Trafford it was a time of wheeling and dealing. The Reds' manager sold Ray Wilkins to AC Milan for £1.5 million and used that money to bring in first Gordon Strachan and Alan Brazil and then Jesper Olsen.

In the chase for Olsen, Atkinson had to compete with interest from the Italians, and Spurs also had him in their sights, but Old Trafford had a trump card: Jesper had been a United fan from boyhood!

Atkinson was rightly excited at the prospect of his new purchase and said at the time: "Jesper Olsen in particular will be a revelation in the English First Division.

"I had received consistently good reports from the Continent about the brilliance of the little Danish player, and his devastating display against England in the European Championship qualifying match confirmed everything I had been told.

"His outstanding skills and total command of the ball ripped England to shreds on that night in Copenhagen. We were treated to a personal confirmation of his rare talent when United played Ajax as part of our preparations for the 1983–84 season.

"My hopes of capturing Olsen were increased considerably when I learned he harboured an ambition to play in English soccer and was a United fanatic," said Atkinson.

"When I met him I was soon deeply impressed by his boyish enthusiasm for the game and the depth of his knowledge on English soccer.

"I am excited by the prospect of what Olsen can achieve in playing for United because I truly believe he has the ability, character and ambition to become the most exciting player seen at Old Trafford since George Best. I am expecting great things from him."

Perhaps the comparison with Best was a tad over the top, but certainly Olsen delivered in his opening season as United won the FA Cup, beating Everton in the final, reaching the quarter-finals of the UEFA Cup and finishing a respectable fourth in the First Division again.

The following season he scored 11 League goals from 25 appearances: mighty good going for a winger and a contribution obviously remembered by United fans, who liked his flair on the wing.

Alex Ferguson took over in 1986 but gradually the Dane seemed to run out of his magic and he was transferred to Bordeaux in 1988 to clear the way for the emergence of wingers Ryan Giggs and Lee Sharpe. He also played for Caen in France, but retained his roots in Manchester where he still lives, working for Proactive, the sports management and marketing firm, with responsibility for the hospitality and events division along with overseas developments in Europe.

PROFILE

BORN Fakse, Denmark
DATE OF BIRTH 20 March 1961
JOINED UNITED July 1984
FEE £500,000
PREVIOUS CLUBS Naestved, Ajax
UNITED LEAGUE APPS 139
GOALS 21
INTERNATIONAL CAPS (Denmark) 43
GOALS 5

"I truly believe he has the ability, character and ambition to become the most exciting player seen at Old Trafford since George Best."

RON ATKINSON ANNOUNCING THE SIGNING OF JESPER OLSEN

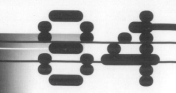

STAN PEARSON

Stan Pearson was not just a master craftsman but also an extremely popular member of Matt Busby's post-war team.

Old team-mates like Johnny Morris and Charlie Mitten not only admired him as probably the most influential member of their star-studded forward line but also as a lovely man.

Johnny Morris says: "Stan was a star. He had a great head on his shoulders. He could send the ball through the tiniest of spaces to make openings for people. He sized up his options in a split second and many people didn't realise just how marvellous he was because he wasn't in the least bit showy. But we all knew. He made it easy for us. He was like a captain of the forward line."

Matt Busby always described Stan as the brains of his attack and indeed he had every attribute of a classic inside-forward: creative, skilful, a superb passer, yet an outstanding goal scorer.

He joined United from school in Salford in 1936, making his debut just before the war aged 17. Service in the 2nd/4th Lancashires robbed him of six years' League football, but he still managed 345 League and FA Cup appearances with a superb return of 149 goals. He put United in front in the 1948 FA Cup final win, after a hat-trick against Derby at Hillsborough to get them to Wembley, and his 22 goals helped win the 1952 Championship.

He was always as complimentary about his colleagues as they were about him, once telling me: "For two or three seasons our forward line picked itself – Delaney, Pearson, Rowley, Morris and Mitten – and we all got to know each other so well that instinctively we knew what was going to happen next. I knew without looking where Jack Rowley would be running. They talk about one-touch football these days as if it is something new, but we were doing it just after the war, and in my opinion no team has done it better."

In all, Stan was associated with United for 17 years, and ironically it was his loyalty which speeded the end of his playing days at Old Trafford, as he recalled for me: "Jimmy Murphy asked me to come with him to Moss Side to talk to a youngster he was trying to sign for United. The problem was that his family were all Manchester City fans and wanted him to go to Maine Road near where they lived. He was an inside-forward, so Jimmy thought that being a first-team inside-forward I might be able to help persuade him to come to United. I had a good chat with him and did my best. At the end of it he did sign for Manchester United … and it was not long before Dennis Viollet took my place in the team!"

After leaving United, Stan moved to Bury and also managed Chester before taking a Post Office and newsagent's in the Cheshire village of Prestbury where he was an unassuming and well-liked member of his local community, remaining active until his death.

PROFILE

BORN Salford
DATE OF BIRTH 11 January 1919
JOINED UNITED December 1935
FEE None
PREVIOUS CLUB Junior
UNITED LEAGUE APPS 315
GOALS 128
INTERNATIONAL CAPS (England) 8
GOALS 5

"They talk about one-touch football these days as if it is something new, but we were doing it just after the war, and in my opinion no team has done it better."

THE LATE STAN PEARSON

RAY WOOD

Have boots, will travel: Ray Wood, the United goalkeeper and Munich survivor, roamed the world to log up an amazing catalogue of jobs after quitting Old Trafford.

When United were winning the European Cup in 1968, Ray was coaching in the USA. Then he had nearly three years in Cyprus, one in Greece, one in Kuwait, four in Kenya and six months in Canada which, along with three and a half years in the United Arab Republic, were topped off with tours for the British Council in Zambia.

He received most of the appointments through recommendations from the Football Association, who knew him as a qualified, reliable and gifted coach – who liked globetrotting!

"I didn't set out to work abroad, but one job just led to another and once I had retired from playing I still needed to work. I enjoyed all the various places, except Greece, where they were too busy selling games and forgetting to pay me, which wasn't much fun.

"I suppose the highspot was in Kenya, where I won the League three times and the Cup once. I also won the Eastern Central National Championship with Kenya in 1975," he said.

United fans, of course, will be more familiar with his life nearer home, after he joined the club from Darlington in 1949 as cover for Jack Crompton.

He earned Championship medals in 1956 and 1957 playing behind the Busby Babes, but it was in the FA Cup that he became part of United folklore, as a central figure in the 1957 drama at Wembley when Aston Villa's Peter McParland crashed into him, leaving him with a broken cheekbone and the dream of a League and Cup double in ruins. The game was only six minutes old. Jackie Blanchflower went into goal and though Ray later came back on United lost 2–1, with McParland ironically the

scorer of the two Villa goals. As Bobby Charlton said in his book: "I cannot believe Villa would have won had we stayed a complete unit, not the way we were playing that season."

Harry Gregg was signed shortly before the Munich crash and took over the goalkeeping position. Ray stayed in the squad, but the dire consequences of the crash with head injuries which hardly helped in his struggle to regain his place.

He moved to Huddersfield in a bid for first-team football and also played for Bradford City and Barnsley before trying his luck in America. And, after qualifying as an FA coach, he spent the next 25 years travelling the world until finally settling at Bexhill in Sussex.

A keen member of the Former Players' Association, he warmly recalls his friendship with Jeff Whitefoot, Dennis Viollet and Mark Jones.

"The four of us used to do the pools, and when one week we came up with 23 points we thought we had won a fortune," he says. "We booked a taxi and a slap-up meal at the Midland Hotel, which for footballers in those days was doing it grand. Matt Busby got to hear about it and sent for us. I think he thought we might not bother with the next game. He needn't have worried. It turned out we had to share £28 and we had to cancel the dinner."

Now retired, golf plays a big part in his life.

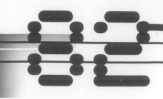

DAVID MAY

You name it, and if it's bad, David May has probably had it.

The Oldham-born defender must rate as one of United's unluckiest player with injuries, and the wonder is that readers of the magazine saw enough of him to vote him into their top 100.

In seven seasons following his £1.25-million transfer from Blackburn Rovers in July 1994 he has been able to make only 65 League starts, and most of those were in his early days as a Red.

The last four years have been a nightmare, but with an astonishing purple patch in the last month of 1998–99 to help land the treble, a sensational finish after months of wondering if he would ever play again.

He had made just two appearances in the Worthington Cup when he reported he was fully fit at

the start of April. He appeared in six League games on the last lap of the Championship, particularly enjoying the final fixture when United beat Spurs 2–1 at Old Trafford to clinch the title.

Six days later he made his one and only appearance in the FA Cup to play at Wembley and collect a medal for his part in the 2–0 victory over Newcastle.

Then it was on to Barcelona and he was on the bench for the Champions' League final against Bayern Munic. He didn't get on, but that didn't stop him leading the celebrations and organising the players as each in turn held up the trophy to a roar from the crowd.

Some of the others who hadn't played looked subdued, but not David May, injury-jinxed for so long and

enjoying every moment of his return to the big time. You couldn't blame him, after a stop-start career with a catalogue of injuries too numerous to list.

He even had to endure a rocky start, unusually, nothing to do with injury. Pressed into playing at right back, it soon became apparent centre-back, his preferred position, was also his best.

He had a particularly uncomfortable game in a defeat against Gothenburg in the European Champions League in his first season which led him to confess: "I am only just beginning to realise how big this club is and there have been times when I have wondered if it is too big for me.

"The fans have not seen the best of me yet. I have been happy with my form when I have played at centre-half. No fears. No worries. That is where I want to play."

May did indeed recover from a rough beginning and though injury-plagued the following season he roared back to become anchorman in defence while, for a change, it was his partners who came and went. He more than deserved his Championship medal.

Alas, two more injury-wrecked seasons were to follow. After his late blaze of treble glory came yet more setbacks – even an injury when he was on loan to Huddersfield – and then he snapped his Achilles tendon. Little wonder he exclaimed: "There is somebody out there who has put a curse on me. Please take it off now because it is doing my head in. It has been a nightmare."

Last season he didn't play at all at senior level and one wonders just what the future holds. At least the supporters have not forgotten his quality when his jinx has allowed him to play, and though it might be scant consolation, he at least figures in United's top hundred, which is no mean achievement.

> ### PROFILE
>
> **BORN** Oldham
> **DATE OF BIRTH** 24 June 1970
> **JOINED UNITED** July 1994
> **FEE** £1.25 million
> **PREVIOUS CLUB** Blackburn Rovers
> **UNITED LEAGUE APPS** 82
> **GOALS** 6
> **INTERNATIONAL CAPS** (England) 0

"There is somebody out there who has put a curse on me. Please take it off now because it is doing my head in. It has been a nightmare."

A HEARTFELT PLEA FROM INJURY-JINXED DAVID MAY

GORDON McQUEEN

There was nothing United fans loved more than the sight of Gordon McQueen on one of his forward charges.

Elbows pumping, knees going, hair flying, his surging run in tune with with the roar of the crowd – perhaps not the most graceful sight in soccer, especially towards the end of his foray, when inevitably he would be somewhat out of control and would either run into someone or simply crash-land.

Then, of course, the bench would start bawling for the 6ft 3ins centre-half to get back to his defensive duties, but the supporters would have none of it. They loved his sprints from one end of the pitch to the other – and when he once nutmegged a defender after careering down the wing, they went wild!

Gordon may not find it flattering to be remembered for his maverick tendencies rather than the quality of his defending , but he can take it for granted everybody respected his normal role and his partnership with Martin Buchan at the heart of the defence.

He gave eight years' good service to Old Trafford and won 30 caps playing for Scotland. It must also be said that not all his raids ended in disaster. He did in fact score 20 League goals, a tally to make, say, Jaap Stam green with envy!

Gordon McQueen was probably Dave Sexton's most influential signing when he went back to Leeds a month after buying Joe Jordan to bring the big man to Old Trafford for £500,000.

The high spots of his United career were three Cup final trips to Wembley; and, after losing to Arsenal in the FA Cup and Liverpool in the Milk Cup, he made it third time lucky with an FA Cup replay victory over Brighton in 1983.

He started his career in Scotland with St Mirren and played there when Archie Knox, later the coach at United as assistant to Sir Alex Ferguson, used

to be a big goal-scorer. He moved into English football with Leeds in a £40,000 transfer marked out as successor to Jack Charlton, a player in the same mould.

He played 150 League games for them, winning a League Championship medal along the way and proving as popular with the Leeds crowd as he was to become with the Old Trafford fans.

After retiring at United, he played and coached in Hong Kong, coming home to Scotland to manage Airdrie and coach St Mirren. He always wanted to break into management, preparing himself by studying the teams and players in the lower divisions where he expected to start. "Anything to stay involved in football," he used to say!

Gordon returned to English football when Bryan Robson was manager of Middlesbrough, becoming his first-team coach, but Steve McClaren's arrival at the Riverside has cast a doubt over his future there.

PROFILE

BORN Kilbirnie, Scotland
DATE OF BIRTH 26 June 1952
JOINED UNITED February 1978
FEE £500,000
PREVIOUS CLUBS Largs, St Mirren, Leeds United
UNITED LEAGUE APPS 184
GOALS 20
INTERNATIONAL CAPS (Scotland) 30
GOALS 5

"Supporters loved his super sprints from one end of the pitch to the other"

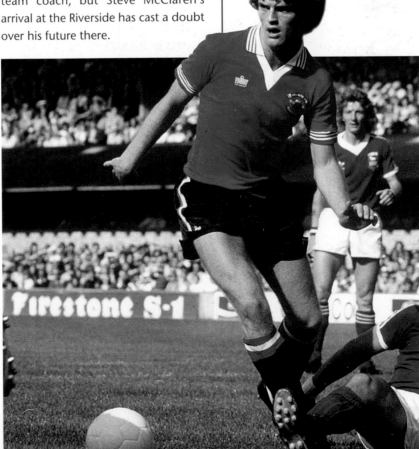

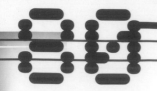

ARNOLD MUHREN

It's a rare club these days which doesn't have a foreign player in its team, but it wasn't always so, and Arnold Muhren was very much a pioneer from overseas in this country in the late Seventies.

It was the enlightened Bobby Robson who brought the Dutchman to England along with compatriot Frans Thijssen. Together they played major roles helping to give Ipswich Town a challenging run in the First Division and in European competition, culminating in a UEFA Cup victory in 1981.

In the summer of 1982, at the end of his contract at Portman Road, the player was entitled to a free transfer as part of his agreement and Ron Atkinson was able to bring him to Old Trafford. He was 31, but without a fee on his head he represented great value and for the next three years gave United a delightful touch in midfield.

"He's a tremendous player and looks so good in our games," said skipper Ray Wilkins. Martin Buchan went even further when he observed: "As a fellow-professional, I think Arnold Muhren is probably the only player in English football I would actually pay to go and watch. He's a sheer joy to see playing."

Ron Atkinson clearly enjoyed watching the Dutchman, too, for he said: "I even find myself clapping at some of the things he does in a game, and that's something a manager just doesn't do –

or didn't before Arnie arrived."

The Dutchman took English football in his stride and I remember him explaining to me: "English football has always had players who have been good in the air and strong in the tackle. The English clubs have had no real need for players in these roles because already there are so many.

"But recently English football has been looking for more technical players and ball-players, like Ardiles, Frans Thijssen and myself, and we have been able to bring something to the game.

"When I first arrived at Ipswich I found they played the English style, with a lot of long balls from the back to the strikers, and they didn't use their midfield people very much. I had been used to having 50 or 60 touches in a game in Holland and at first at Ipswich I was lucky to get 20. I wondered what on earth I was doing in England.

"Ipswich were a team in a hurry until they brought Frans to help me in midfield, and eventually we played a more Continental style. We were always in the top five, and of course we played in Europe. Now I hope I can fit in at Manchester United."

He certainly did, and at the end of his first season helped win the FA Cup, scoring a penalty in the final replay against Brighton at Wembley. He also collected a Milk Cup finalist's medal.

In 1984–85 injuries brought his United career to a close, but back in Holland he made a remarkable recovery to play for Ajax in the final of the 1987 European Cup Winners' Cup. Then, the following year, at the age of 37, he helped Holland to win the European Championship.

PROFILE

BORN Vollendam, Holland
DATE OF BIRTH 2 June 1951
JOINED UNITED August 1982
FEE None
PREVIOUS CLUBS Ajax, FC Twente, Ipswich Town
UNITED LEAGUE APPS 70
GOALS 13
INTERNATIONAL CAPS (Holland) 23
GOALS 3

"As a fellow-professional, I think Arnold Muhren is probably the only player in English football I would actually pay to go and watch. He's a sheer joy to see playing."

MARTIN BUCHAN

MAURICE SETTERS

United fans were stunned when their team crashed to a 7–3 defeat at Newcastle United in January 1960 as Munich's savage impact on playing resources made its presence felt again.

The shock result upset the United-supporting editor of the *Manchester Evening News,* Tom Henry, so much that he secretly changed the headline which had been prepared, announcing in big letters that the Reds had been thrashed. The Pink that night came out instead with a much more fan-friendly head-line: "United in 10-goal thriller".

Henry, a friend of Matt Busby, natu-rally found his new version more acceptable, but it did nothing to deter the manager from what he knew had to be done.

It was his team's third defeat in a fortnight and immediately he moved in for Maurice Setters, paying West Bromwich Albion £30,000. Setters had something of a reputation for rugged play which some thought wouldn't have suited Busby, but it was a situation calling for drastic action and the trans-fer proved successful, with the midfield considerably stronger for his tough-tackling presence.

It wasn't a particularly successful time, as the club suffered the after-effects of the Munich crash, and he played a key role in pulling United through the ravages of the disaster. Indeed, he was instrumental in taking them to Wembley in 1963 for their FA Cup final success against Leicester City.

Setters was a natural leader and cap-tained the club for a period. He was never shy of putting his thoughts into words – as I can personally testify, after having been on the receiving end a good few times when he took issue with some of my reports.

It was perhaps his outspoken hon-esty which helped end his career at Old Trafford. At one stage, the youthful Nobby Stiles was on the point of a transfer to Wolves after taking the view that as understudy to Setters it would take too long to displace him in the team.

Maurice, however, advised him to stay and battle it out, which is exactly what he did, and so successfully that it wasn't long before he had taken his mentor's position.

Setters moved to Stoke 18 months after the Cup success and then played for Coventry and Charlton to make a career total of more than 500 senior games.

He won 16 caps with the England Under-23 team and was unlucky to miss full honours. A combination of his physical commitment and injuries meant he finished his career with knees so badly damaged that he was left bandy-legged.

Happily a procedure called "Oxford knee", inserting plastic cartilages, straightened him up, to leave the always-cheerful Maurice telling me: "I must be at least an inch taller now."

He was a natural for management and did well at Doncaster where he eventually settled his family. He also worked in various capacities for Sheffield Wednesday, Rotherham and Newcastle. His most successful period in management, though, came as assistant to Jack Charlton with the Republic of Ireland team. Together they breathed new life into the talented but inconsistent Irish players, inspir-ing them to a memorable 1–0 victory over England in the European Championships of 1988 in Germany.

PROFILE

BORN Honiton, Devon
DATE OF BIRTH 16 December 1936
JOINED UNITED January 1960
FEE £30,000
PREVIOUS CLUBS Exeter City, West Bromwich Albion
UNITED LEAGUE APPS 159
GOALS 12
INTERNATIONAL CAPS (England) 0 (Under-23) 16

"He was never shy of putting his thoughts into words – as I can testify, having been on the receiving end a good few times."

Born at Honiton in Devon, Setters had begun his career with Exeter City but was snapped up by West Bromwich after only 10 League games. He spent five years in the Midlands before Busby took him to Old Trafford for a contri-bution that makes him a worthy Great.

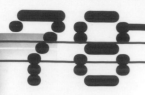

MARK JONES

"He was a big, fine lad. Everybody loved him. He was everything you would want your own son to be. As a footballer, he had great stature, tremendous in the air, and he was a great passer of the ball."

JOHN DOHERTY

Mark Jones came from Barnsley and played in the same England Boys' team as Dennis Viollet and Jeff Whitefoot.

A well-built boy, his obvious potential as a defender made him a target for a number of clubs, with United winning the race for his signature in June 1948. He was then 15, and gave up work as a bricklayer's apprentice to cross the Pennines.

He was still only 17 when Matt Busby gave him his League debut in October 1950 in a 3–1 win at Old Trafford against Sheffield Wednesday. He was the pathfinder as the manager started to introduce his Busby Babes, but he still had a long time to wait before he could count on a regular first-team place.

In fact it took Mark four more years to establish himself in the team because the man in front of him at centre-half was Allenby Chilton, the captain and a commanding figure.

However, when he did oust the captain towards the end of season 1954–55, he made the position his own and was an ever-present the following year to help win the Championship.

It was a smooth transition, because just as Chilton had been magnificent in the air playing as a traditional centre-half, so Jones took over with the same brand of confident and powerful command.

It was widely acknowledged that the Championship half-back line of Eddie Colman, Jones and Duncan Edwards was easily the best in the country. Mind you, such was the competition for places, with a seemingly endless supply

of Busby Babes entering the scene, that near the end of the next season he lost his place to Jackie Blanchflower, another fine centre-half, who kept him out for almost an entire year and meant that he missed playing in the 1957 final of the FA Cup.

It was a fierce competition, with Blanchflower edging his rival as the more skilful but Jones a fraction more commanding. Mark regained his place in the weeks leading up to the Munich air crash and was in the team which played Red Star Belgrade to qualify for the European Cup semi-finals before the tragic flight home.

Who would eventually have won the fight for a place is anybody's guess and both Jones and Blanchflower more than deserve their ranking in the Greats. What is beyond dispute when you talk to Mark's contemporaries is their respect for a most likeable man.

John Doherty, who won a Championship medal with him in 1956, says: "He was a big, fine lad, but the thing is everyone loved him. He used to wear a trilby, which was unusual for a young man in those days, and he would puff on the pipe he smoked.

"He was everything you would want your own son to be. As a footballer he had this great stature, tremendous in the air, and he was a precise passer of the ball. Like Allenby Chilton, the man he took over from, he didn't take many prisoners.

"His rival for a place, Jackie Blanchflower, perhaps had more flair and I don't know which of them would have come out on top had Mark been spared at Munich and Jackie had not been so badly injured that he was unable to play again."

One thing for sure is that he would have gone on to play for England.

REMI MOSES

When Ron Atkinson arrived as manager of Manchester United in 1981 he was full of praise for the attacking stars he found at Old Trafford like Frank Stapleton and Lou Macari.

He also liked the quality at the back with defenders such as Martin Buchan and Gordon McQueen, but lamented to me in his early days: "Who on earth is going to stop the opposition streaming at us through the middle?"

The answer, of course, was, "Not a lot", because while there were creative players in midfield like Ray Wilkins, there weren't many ball-winners. The result was an SOS for determined tacklers to shore up a soft centre and Atkinson immediately went back to his old club, West Bromwich Albion, with £2 million to sign Bryan Robson and Remi Moses. Though Robson attracted most publicity, Moses' value should not be overlooked, and it is significant that the little guy has not been forgotten by the Greats' voters!

An unassuming young man quite content to let Robson have the limelight, Moses was a gritty midfielder who answered perfectly Atkinson's requirements. He was a bantam in size, but deadly at winning the ball and would have made a more lasting impression for both club and country but for a catalogue of injuries and a suspect ankle.

Moses was returning to his roots as a one-time Stretford End fan. Growing up in the tough Miles Platting area where the local shale soccer pitch was known as "the Red Rec", he had played Sunday soccer as well as for Manchester Boys, but despite this there were no takers locally, and it was left to Johnny Giles to sign him on at West Bromwich.

Ron Atkinson became an admirer when he took over at The Hawthorns and later said: "I called him my lucky mascot. When I put Remi in the team at the Albion, we were down near the bottom of the League. We lost only one of the next 18 games he played. Then after I had signed him for United and we hadn't won a game, we climbed right to the top. He is a lad who never stopped working, never gave less than a hundred per cent and did a hell of a lot for the players around him."

Remi learned the lesson as a youngster that you can't play if you don't have the ball. Perhaps reflecting the era in which he played, he said, "Being small had something to do with the way I battled. Maybe it was tougher growing up as a black kid in an area like Miles Platting. I wouldn't know. It was a struggle for everyone. I didn't notice a lot of racial tension among the kids of my age. Perhaps there was with the older lads. The only thing is, when you're black and somebody decides to have a go at you, that's the first word that comes out of his mouth."

His partnership with Robson flourished and he earned England Under-21 honours, but never had much luck. Suspension cost him a place in the 1983 FA Cup final and an ankle injury put him out of the 1985 final, probably also denying him the full international honours his club form merited.

He was at Old Trafford for three more seasons but injuries became an increasing problem and he was never able to get a decent run of games.

He survived into the Alex Ferguson era but was forced to retire in 1988 and, true to character, slipped back quietly into life in Manchester with little more contact with the club, despite repeated invitations from Sir Alex to come and see them and perhaps train a little with them.

PROFILE

BORN Manchester
DATE OF BIRTH 14 November 1960
JOINED UNITED September 1981
FEE (estimated value) £625,000
PREVIOUS CLUB West Bromwich Albion
UNITED LEAGUE APPS 150
GOALS 7

"He is a lad who never stopped working, never gave less than a hundred per cent and did a hell of a lot for the players around him."

RON ATKINSON

JACK CROMPTON

Come 65 and most men, even top sports achievers, are ready to put their feet up and take life a bit easier.

PROFILE

BORN Manchester
DATE OF BIRTH 18 December 1921
JOINED UNITED June 1944
FEE None
PREVIOUS CLUBS Goslings
UNITED LEAGUE APPS 191
GOALS 0

"There might be some argument about who was the best goalkeeper in the country, but there was none about who was the fittest."

TEAM-MATE JOHNNY MORRIS

Few pensioners are to be found in track suits running groups of not necessarily very talented youngsters round a training pitch, perhaps in pouring rain and freezing cold.

But then Jack Crompton, United goalkeeper and coach, was always different. Fitness for him was more a way of life than a discipline to be endured. The result was that after a working life dedicated to training, pensionable age made no difference and Jack was still to be found taking evening sessions as one of the coaches employed in community sport at the Platt Lane complex in Moss Side.

Manchester City use the centre during the day and then it is turned over to amateur footballers, and even hockey players, who can hire not only the all-weather pitch but a qualified coach to get them fit and develop their skills.

Working with these local youngsters was a far cry from honing the silky skills of Manchester United stars, but Jack lost none of his enthusiasm – and woe betide any youngsters who felt pensioner Crompton was no longer capable of lasting the pace. Many a lad was left gasping trying to keep up with Jack Crompton in his favourite feet-raising and sit-up exercise.

Maintaining an interest in youth sport long after finishing in the professional game perhaps stemmed from his own early days when he was a keen member of the YMCA and a walking and climbing enthusiast, as well as a keen amateur goalkeeper.

He played for the local amateur club Goslings, a works team, joining United in 1944 and making his League debut just after the war. He was reliability personified in Sir Matt Busby's first team which won the FA Cup in 1948.

His highlight in the Wembley final was stopping a piledriver from Stan Mortensen 11 minutes from the end with the scores at 2–2 and then mounting his own attack with a long clearance to find Stan Pearson, who streaked away to put United ahead and on their way to a handsome 4–2 victory.

Jack went on to make over 200 League appearances before losing his place to Reg Allen, signed from QPR. He regained it, but lost out again when Ray Wood was signed from Darlington.

He left to become trainer at Luton in 1956 but two years later responded to the Munich crash emergency by returning to Old Trafford to help Jimmy Murphy put the club back together in their hour of need. Solid as a rock, Jack was there right through the success of the Sixties until after Sir Matt Busby retired, and went into management himself at Barrow.

He coached for Bobby Charlton at Preston and was at Bury before returning to Old Trafford for a third spell in 1974 as part of Tommy Docherty's backroom staff.

Always unassuming and full of common sense, he brought to his long career as a trainer the qualities he had as a player, best summed up by team-mate Johnny Morris when he said, "There might be some argument about who was the best goalkeeper in the country, but there was none about who was the fittest.

"Crompo would train most of the day with the lads before popping round to the YMCA for a bit more work, then head up into the hills for an evening stroll.

"He never let us down. We played on some poor pitches and with a bumpy old ball, but Crompo didn't make silly mistakes."

Jack retired to Tenerife, where he played tennis every day, but is now back living in the Manchester area.

CHARLIE MITTEN

Charlie Mitten was one of the great characters of the post-war era, as well as possessing what his contemporaries would describe as the sweetest left foot in the business.

They reckoned he could drop a centre on a sixpence, and as for penalty-taking John Doherty, the one-time Busby Babe, remembers: "United beat Aston Villa 7–0 at Old Trafford and Charlie Mitten scored three of his four goals with penalties. He hit the right-hand stanchion with his first and the left-hand one with his second. Then with the third he asked the goalkeeper which one he wanted this time. The keeper pointed and Charlie obliged, with the goalkeeper still powerless to do anything about it."

There is no doubt he turned left-wing play into an art form, yet he was also something of a rebel. He joined the club straight from school in 1936 and was ready for his senior debut when war broke out. After serving as an RAF PT instructor, he picked up his career again to help win the FA Cup in 1948. Then his sense of adventure took over and on a tour of the Americas he was invited to play for Santa Fé in Colombia for a £10,000 signing-on fee and a weekly wage of £60 – very tempting when the winter wage at home was £8, dropping to £6 in summer.

As Charlie maintained, "I'd never seen that much money in my life before. If I had stayed with United for 25 years I'd never have made anything like it. I could have bought a row of houses with what the Colombians were paying. It was an irresistible offer." So off he went, in the footsteps of Neil Franklin, the England and Stoke centre-half. Unfortunately Colombia was outside FIFA, so on his return after a year he was suspended and United had to transfer-list him after only four seasons.

The self-styled "Bogata Bandit" was sold for £20,000 to Fulham and played there for five years before becoming player-manager at Mansfield. Then he was appointed manager at Newcastle where he indulged his passion for dog-racing. It was said he had a hotline from his office at St James's Park to the track and sometimes brought favoured dogs into the ground for medical treatment.

Eventually returning to Manchester, he managed the White City dog track before turning to sports promotion, specialising in arranging tours abroad.

There was no doubt he made a big impact in Colombia, because Real Madrid signed Santa Fé's two Argentineans, Alfredo di Stefano and Hector Rial, and wanted Charlie to go to Madrid as well. He could easily have become part of the Real Madrid side which dominated Europe at that time, winning the European Cup for five successive seasons after its inception, but a wife who preferred to come home and the need to educate his children brought him back to a six-month ban and £250 fine. His adventure blighted his international career, as Sir Stanley Rous, secretary of the FA at the time, explained: "We know you are the best outside-left in the country, but I'm afraid we can't select you for England because discipline must come first."

His two boys, John and Charles, both subsequently played for United.

In later years di Stefano, the maestro who so impressed United when they met in the European Cup, told him: "Ah, Charlee Meeton, numero uno. If we have heem, we never need Gento. Gento, he queek but Meeton, he more clever." As Charlie, not in the best of health these days, reflected: "Nice of him to say so – and it does make you wonder!"

"I could have bought a row of houses with what the Colombians were paying. It was an irresistible offer.'
CHARLIE MITTEN ON THE DEAL WHICH CHANGED HIS LIFE

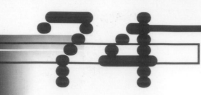

RAIMOND VAN DER GOUW

The girls in the office at Old Trafford call him Raimond van der Gorgeous!

Not for nothing, either – he's a good-looking fellow with charm to match – but then he's no ordinary footballer. It takes a special personality to accept so patiently and for so long the role of reserve goalkeeper.

First it was Peter Schmeichel and then Fabien Barthez, as he loyally waited on the bench; training, always training, playing sometimes in the reserves and occasionally the first team. Is it lack of ambition or is life simply too good with United, even as an understudy?

Signed from Vitesse Arnhem in 1996 for £200,000, in the full knowledge he was unlikely to displace Schmeichel, I put it to him that it must be a frustrating life, but he replied: "My last contract was for another two years and I would have signed for longer if I had been able because this is a wonderful club, one of the biggest in the world.

"I knew what I was coming to and I accepted it. Clearly the Boss is happy with my contribution or he would not have offered me a further agreement at Old Trafford. I took my new contract as showing a lot of respect for me.

"And because I am the second goalkeeper doesn't mean I take it easy. I have to be fit and sharp all the time because I never know when I will be called on.

"It's always difficult to provide top cover because the chances don't come very often. There is big pressure and then it's all over. It's not easy but I have been satisfied with my performances and though I haven't been called on very often, I am always very busy.

'I took over from Alan Hodgkinson as the club's goalkeeping coach for a time and I enjoyed the teaching side. For 10 years in Holland I was a part-time PE teacher for youngsters between six and 12 years old and I also studied for coaching qualifications.

"This is what I want to do in the future, coaching, and perhaps specialised goalkeeping work. Whether it is in England or back home in Holland will depend on where I can get a job.

"I knew right from the start that I would only be in the first team through injury. Of course, if I were 20 years old I would agree with you that it would be very frustrating, but I was 33 when I came to Manchester and at that age it would have been difficult to find a club as big as United.

"But say I did find one; how long would I be the first goalkeeper? Perhaps after a while at my age I would be a number two again, and if I am going to be a reserve, I would prefer to be one at United. I like it in England. My wife and two children are settled."

It's got to be said that van der Gouw has never let the side down when he has played. He is popular with the crowd who clearly admire his loyalty as well as his 'keeping, which of course is why he was voted into the Greats.

PROFILE

BORN Oldenzaal, Holland
DATE OF BIRTH 14 March 1963
JOINED UNITED July 1996
FEE £200,000
PREVIOUS CLUB Vitesse Arnhem
UNITED LEAGUE APPS 36
GOALS 0
INTERNATIONAL CAPS 0

> "My last contract was for another two years and I would have signed for longer if I had been able because this is a wonderful club. I took my new contract as showing a lot of respect for me."
>
> RAIMOND VAN DER GOUW

JOHN ASTON SNR

Big John Aston, described in that way to separate him from his son of the same name, is part of an exclusive family double.

Father won a Championship medal in 1952 and John Aston junior achieved the same honour in 1967. There have been other famous father-and-son double-acts, like Alec and David Herd who played together for Stockport County, and many boys follow their dads into professional football, but as far as I know the Astons are the only father and son to win First Division titles playing for the same club.

John senior was a dependable member of Sir Matt Busby's first team, sharing in the FA Cup success of 1948 and then collecting a Championship medal four years later.

As a schoolboy he played on the old grounds at Newton Heath and Bank Street in Clayton before signing for United as an amateur in 1937, a product of the MUJACs, the Manchester United Junior Athletic Club, forerunner of youth development at Old Trafford. He had hardly got started, though, when war broke out and he joined the Royal Marines to see service abroad as a Commando. He didn't become a professional until he was demobbed, when he quickly established himself as a regular in the first team. Like Johnny Carey, he started life as an inside-forward and was converted to full-back by Busby to form a great partnership with Carey.

John was the only player to be an ever-present in both the Cup and League in the 1948 season. Although playing in defence, he was often switched to the attack with telling effect to help cover an injury or rescue a difficult situation.

He never lost his attacking ideas, and in season 1950–51, after being moved to centre-forward for the second half of the season, he scored 15 League goals. He became a regular England international to win 17 caps.

He played his last match in 1954, his retirement hastened by illness along with the emergence of the Busby Babes, a development he accepted, though perhaps a little reluctantly.

"It was very disappointing for the players who had brought the Championship to Old Trafford for the first time in 40 years to have to give way to the new men, but we were not blind to the fact that the Boss had also been busy creating a tremendously successful youth team, winning the FA Youth Cup five times off the reel when it was inaugurated," he explained.

"Matt Busby had been long enough at the club, though, to have established himself as a very far-seeing and shrewd manager.

"He had won the respect of us all, which meant it was easier for him to put over his new ideas. Matt Busby was an amazing man. He was kind, he was gentle, but he could also be very strong and firm."

Freddie Goodwin, the former United player, had Aston at Birmingham City as a scout at the end of his playing career, but he returned to Old Trafford after the Munich crash to become a junior coach. He was the chief scout, though, when Frank O'Farrell was sacked, and failed to survive an extensive purge.

His departure was bitter and resented for a long time afterwards, after 35 years' service for the club as player, coach and scout. He joined the family pet food business and has lately been in failing health.

PROFILE

BORN Manchester
DATE OF BIRTH 3 September 1921
JOINED UNITED January 1938
FEE None
PREVIOUS CLUB MUJAC
UNITED LEAGUE APPS 253
GOALS 29
INTERNATIONAL CAPS (England) 17
GOALS 0

"John Aston senior was a dependable member of Sir Matt Busby's first team, sharing in the FA Cup success of 1948 and then collecting a Championship medal four years later."

DAVID PEGG

David Pegg's story told you everything about the quality of the Busby Babes and the fact that there were so many of them jostling for places in the first team.

Sir Matt Busby was indeed spoilt for choice in those heady days before the Munich air crash decimated their ranks in the most appalling way.

Though he had had a scintillating junior career and had made a stunning impact at senior level, for both United and England, the fact was that Pegg had lost his place to Albert Scanlon in the weeks leading up to the disaster.

He was not the only one, of course. Billy Whelan was also out of the side as Bobby Charlton arrived on the scene, young Kenny Morgans had replaced Johnny Berry and Jackie Blanchflower had given way to Mark Jones.

They were still in the squad, of course, and they were all on the trip to Red Star Belgrade. But, given David Pegg's pedigree, Scanlon had done extraordinarily well to squeeze him out of the side.

David won five caps for England schoolboys and was a much sought-after youngster, with chief scout Joe Armstrong a regular visitor to Doncaster. He crossed the Pennines in September 1950 and immediately became a star of the youth team at inside-left, with Scanlon his winger.

Together they helped destroy Wolves, especially in the 7–1 first leg win of the FA Youth Cup final in 1953, and repeated their class act the following year, albeit by a closer margin, but with a hat-trick from David.

Busby gave him his League debut at Middlesbrough when he had just turned 17, and Pegg continued his international career with Under-23 appearances.

He flourished on the European scene, making a particular impression when United made their debut in the European Cup in a preliminary round against Anderlecht in 1956.

The Reds beat the Belgians 2–0 in the first leg and then ran riot to win 10–0 at Maine Road.

Jimmy Murphy later wrote in his memoirs: "The only forward who didn't score was David Pegg, who skated over the mud like a man on water-skis, creating the openings for at least five of the goals, while his team-mates tried desperately to give him the goal he so richly deserved."

The occasion was fondly remembered by the player as well, and he later wrote: "I shall never forget the night our forward line really clicked, the night when everybody did everything right except me. I couldn't score. We played the best football we have ever played. Dennis Viollet scored four, Tommy Taylor three, Billy Whelan two, Johnny Berry one. Near the end they all tried to tee one up for me, but the ball just wouldn't go in."

Normally scoring wasn't too difficult for him, with a record of 28 in 148 appearances in the League and four from 12 in Europe, good going for a flying winger whose great talent was crossing the ball.

He played once for the full England team, against the Republic of Ireland in 1957, and there is every reason to think he would have added to that tally but for the tragedy of Munich cutting him down, still aged only 22.

PROFILE

BORN Doncaster
DATE OF BIRTH 20 September 1935
JOINED UNITED September 1950
FEE None
PREVIOUS CLUB Junior
UNITED LEAGUE APPS 127
GOALS 24
INTERNATIONAL CAPS (England) 1
GOALS 0

"There is every reason to think he would have added to his international tally but for the tragedy of Munich cutting him down at 22."

PAUL PARKER

He didn't often catch your eye, but then there wasn't much of him at 5ft 7ins, and as Sir Alex Ferguson said, "He was one of those players you never really noticed because he was so efficient and good at his job. We didn't lose too many matches when he was playing."

The United manager made his move for Parker in 1991 while he was on a pre-season tour in Norway and heard that Everton were bidding for the QPR full-back. He asked the chairman to inquire whether the player would be willing to talk to United, and after going to see both Arsenal and Spurs he travelled up to Old Trafford.

Ferguson is convinced that it was a group of United fans who swung the £1.7-million transfer United's way.

"We went out into the stand and there were about 300 supporters sitting there. They just seemed to be watching the grass grow and one of them shouted: 'Are you signing, Paul?' Straight away he called back: 'Yes, I'm signing.' I'm convinced it helped him make up his mind."

His first season was dogged by various injuries, and he later said: "To be honest, I felt a bit of a fraud to be calling myself a Manchester United player. It seemed I was an outsider because I was never in the team for the vital times. I felt the fans didn't look on me as one of them. I didn't blame them because they didn't see enough of me."

But he fought back to claim the right-back position in the team which ended the long wait for the Championship in season 1992–93, and he was a regular member of the double-winning team the following year.

"I was at Old Trafford when it all kicked off," he said. "Since then they have won a few Championships but that first one was special to anyone involved. It was the first for me and the first for United for 26 years. I am very proud of my medals."

He had two more seasons at Old Trafford but the best days were behind him as injuries struck again and the emerging Gary Neville increasingly claimed his position.

He left in 1996 on a whirlwind tour, playing in quick succession for Derby County, Sheffield United, Fulham and Chelsea before non-League football with Heybridge Swifts and Farnborough.

At his peak for United, Sir Alex Ferguson reckoned he was the key who locked the defence together and Peter Schmeichel commented at the time, "Just nothing is getting through from his side of the field."

London-born, he began his career as an apprentice at Fulham before moving to Queens Park Rangers where he won the first of 19 caps for England at centre-half, his preferred position in his early days.

He settled in the South at the end of his career to run his car-leasing company in Hendon and run the Brentwood wine bar he opened when he was a United player. We still see him in Manchester, though, with his work for United's television station.

"That first Championship is special to anyone involved. I am very proud of my medals."
PAUL PARKER

JIM HOLTON

PROFILE

BORN Lesmahagow, Scotland
DATE OF BIRTH 11 April 1951
JOINED UNITED January 1973
FEE £80,000
PREVIOUS CLUBS West Bromwich Albion, Shrewsbury Town
UNITED LEAGUE APPS 63
GOALS 5
INTERNATIONAL CAPS
(Scotland) 15
GOALS 2

He was a ball of fire with a strapping build and athleticism to go with it. Not for nothing did United fans in the early '70s chant: "Six foot two, eyes of blue, Big Jim Holton's after you."

Later it was learned he had always had a heart problem. You wouldn't have guessed it, because he flung himself into the game with such enthusiasm, perhaps because he was, relatively speaking, an overnight success.

As he said himself, "Everything happened so quickly for me. One day I was

> "One day I was playing for Shrewsbury in the Third Division and then suddenly I was at Manchester United, and that was only the beginning."
>
> JIM HOLTON ON HIS METEORIC RISE TO FOOTBALLING FAME

playing for Shrewsbury in the Third Division and then suddenly I was at Manchester United, and that was only the beginning. After only another two months I was playing for the Scotland Under-21 team and by the end of the season I was trotting out at Wembley to play for the full Scotland team against England."

The man who set him on the road to success was Harry Gregg, the former United goalkeeper, when he was manager of Shrewsbury. He picked him up after he had failed to make the grade with West Bromwich Albion and persuaded him to play to his strengths using his size, his strength and his natural command in the air.

Jim, with his confidence restored by his new manager, prospered and 18 months later Tommy Docherty took him for a modest £80,000. He was the perfect player for the Doc's swashbuckling team as they went down to

the Second Division, only to come roaring back up at the first attempt.

He wasn't a showman, nor did he play to the gallery, but the supporters loved him. Their team were up against it and somehow Holton expressed the kind of fighting spirit they appreciated was needed at the time.

His popularity always seemed to take the player by surprise. "The punters were unbelievable," he once told me. "I still don't know why, but they really seemed to take to me. They had this rhyme about me and I had a tremendous rapport. I have to be honest and say I loved it, but it was always a bit strange. Let's face it, I wasn't gifted like some of the other players. I can only think that they perhaps liked the fact that I always gave a hundred per cent.

"They were a different class and I was lucky, because if they didn't fancy you, they could be very cruel. I saw that happen as well, but happily I enjoyed a good relationship and I think my best moment of all at Old Trafford was when the fans voted me their Player of the Year in season 1973–74."

He was right to enjoy his time at Old Trafford because it didn't last long. He broke his leg playing in the Second Division at Sheffield Wednesday and then again in a comeback with the reserves. By the time he was fit again, Docherty had turned against him and sold him to Sunderland. He later moved on to Coventry, put down roots and became landlord of the Rising Sun.

He won 15 Scottish caps and made 63 League appearances, not a lot in comparison with some others, but nobody made a bigger impact in as short a time.

As Martin Buchan says: "He was a great bloke and a great player, popular with the players as well as with the fans."

Watching Jim Holton in action it would have been impossible to imagine that by the age of 41 he would die from a heart attack.

HENNING BERG

Henning Berg says he got a rude awakening when he was transferred from Blackburn Rovers to Manchester United in August 1997.

"I knew when I came that I wouldn't be playing in all the games, but what I didn't know was how I would feel about not playing regularly in the first team and it turned out I didn't know how to handle it," he explained.

"I think at Blackburn I took being in the team all the time a little bit for granted and I didn't appreciate it.

"Then even though I knew it wouldn't be like that at Old Trafford, because there is so much competition and so many good players, I found it very frustrating.

"All my career I had been a first-team regular and when I was made a substitute at United it was my first experience of being on the bench.

"I didn't handle the situation very well and when I was out for a spell I felt upset and dissatisfied.

"I also found it difficult when I got a chance again because of the pressure of knowing that I would have to play well and settle in straight away if I was to stay in the side. Eventually, I came to terms with the battle for places and took it a game at a time.

"I stopped worrying about what would happen for the next match and I tried to appreciate it more when I was actually in the team without worrying about the situation so much."

Henning Berg neatly sums up the frustrations and demands of playing at Old Trafford, where all but very few have to deal with Sir Alex Ferguson's rotation system and his determination to make full use of his pool of quality players.

Some take it in their stride, others struggle to come to terms with it , and Berg felt the full pressure of a central defensive department packed with very able and experienced players.

There was no denying his ability, however. He played 159 League games for Blackburn and earned a Championship medal with them in 1995 as well as winning the Norwegian Player of the Year title.

He had also impressed playing for Norway with more than 50 caps, often in partnership with Ronny Johnsen, and the United manager paid Blackburn £5 million for him in the close season of 1997.

Berg's first appearance was as a substitute for his Norwegian team-mate against Southampton a few days later, and emerging from a bout of injuries he had an outstanding year to help achieve the 1999 treble.

His performances in Europe were especially notable in a solid partnership with Jaap Stam.

He was brilliant in the quarter-final 1–1 draw against Inter Milan in Italy, and who will forget his marvellous clearance off the line when a goal seemed certain in the first-leg win against Inter at Old Trafford?

The following season saw him start well in the continued absence of the injured Johnsen, but an uncertain display against Fiorentina in Italy undermined his confidence and the pressure built up again with the arrival of Mikael Silvestre.

Early in season 2000–01 he was quietly transferred back to Blackburn, but once again he flourished to win promotion and bring the Rovers back into the Premiership.

> "Eventually I came to terms with the battle for places and learned to take it a game at a time."
>
> HENNING BERG ON THE ROTATION SYSTEM

JOHN ASTON JNR

John Aston's place in the Greats is undoubtedly linked with one of the club's great moments: the day they beat Benfica at Wembley to become the first English club to win the European Cup.

PROFILE

BORN Manchester
DATE OF BIRTH 28 June 1947
JOINED UNITED June 1963
FEE None
PREVIOUS CLUB Junior
UNITED LEAGUE APPS 253
GOALS 29
INTERNATIONAL CAPS 0

> "It is one of the few things in my life that never diminishes with time. It was Matt Busby's and Manchester United's greatest night."
>
> JOHN ASTON JNR ON BEATING BENFICA

It's perhaps a little harsh to imply that John's greatness stemmed from just one match, because he was an important member of the team which had won the League Championship the season before to qualify for a second crack at Europe in the Sixties.

The son of a United star and later a youth coach, John Aston senior, he had a sparkling run right through the season leading up to the European tri-umph. He made 34 League appearances and scored 10 goals, a useful tally for a man who patrolled the left flank in the manner of an orthodox winger.

At the same time, it has got to be his performance at Wembley which lingers in the memory because he turned on so much style and pace against Adolfo, the luckless Benfica right-back, that in many people's eyes he was man of the match.

As Bobby Charlton puts it, "Johnny Aston had a particularly good game, running the legs off their full-back to produce some great crosses. He pulled their defence wide, which gave the rest of us more room."

It was certainly a rewarding experience for young John because not all the fans appreciated his style, and at times had not been slow to express their displeasure. His problem was that he was playing in an attack featuring three European Footballers of the Year in Charlton, Law and Best. Who wouldn't look a little ordinary at times in comparison? As he says himself: "For me, it was a bit like being a workhorse alongside thoroughbreds. It did get to me, and at times I had tremendous problems with the crowd."

On the occasion of the final, though, everything came right just when it mattered most and he says now: "It is one of the few things in my life that never diminishes with time. I remember the George Best goal, a great Alex Stepney save and I can remember playing well. But they were all very secondary to what it all meant. It was Matt Busby's and Manchester United's greatest night. That's what makes me very proud."

His other memory is more personal. "We wore blue in the final, and blue is a good colour for the Astons. My dad wore a blue shirt when he won an FA Cup medal with United in 1948," he explained.

All quite humble words, but then that is typical of a modest and unassuming man who at the end of his career was quite content to return to the family pet shop business.

His career at Old Trafford was set back by a broken leg the season after the European success and in 1972 he was transferred to Luton, later playing for Mansfield and Blackburn.

He was pleased with United's more recent European success in the Champions League, and perhaps the massive time gap of 31 years points up the merit of his own big day.

As he succinctly puts it, "People look at me now, a bald-headed man with a beard, and it reminds them just how long it is since we did it. It was about time."

WILLIE MORGAN

Willie Morgan's career at Old Trafford was a bumpy ride that often seemed in crisis.

He arrived with high hopes when Matt Busby made him his first signing after winning the European Cup in 1968, paying Burnley £100,000 as he set out to rebuild what was clearly a team growing a little long in the tooth.

Morgan was only 24 and had been an accomplished right winger at Turf Moor and for Scotland, a player with a trick or two for beating full-backs, good acceleration and a nice line in crossing.

Little did Willie Morgan guess the roller-coaster trip that lay ahead after Sir Matt had retired, however. First Wilf McGuinness and then Frank O'Farrell tried to steady the ship but they only got 18 months apiece in the job.

Morgan admitted at the time: "I can't honestly say I regretted joining United, but there were times in my first few seasons that my confidence was at a low ebb. In fact there was a time when Wilf McGuinness was manager that I thought of packing in the game. He made it plain he didn't fancy me as a player and I made it plain that the feeling was mutual.

"Things improved when Frank O'Farrell took over but even with Frank I had some differences of opinion. When our luck ran out Frank was too aloof. The spirit in the club went and there was nothing he seemed able to do about it."

But then Tommy Docherty breezed in and though he couldn't prevent relegation he lit Morgan's fire, made him his captain and resurrected his international career. The Doc said at the time: "I have seen Willie in action at all levels now. When I had him in Brazil with Scotland he was voted the best outside-right in the whole tournament. For his club, despite relegation, he has shown a consistency that has been incredible. Week in and week out he gives such a

lot to his game. His stamina matches his skill. When he has finished in football he could always become a marathon runner. His stamina is fantastic.

"I cannot think of a better player in his position in English football, nor in the world. He is a great professional and a great competitor," he added.

Willie said simply: "I am biased where Tom is concerned. To me, the man is magic. He is a great motivator."

But within a few months of being back in the First Division, manager and player were at loggerheads. The manager started to leave Willie out of the team to make way for Steve Coppell.

Some of the fans didn't like it and got up a petition suggesting that their hero was being victimised. But the Doc, never averse to a good player confrontation, would have none of it. Matters came to a head at the end of the season with Docherty's claim that Morgan didn't want to go on the club's summer trip to Australia bringing the player's wife storming into the fray.

"I'm just about sick of it. Willie is being driven into asking for a move," she declared.

It was all good knockabout stuff for the papers, ending in a spectacular court case with a slanging match between manager and player. Morgan went back to Burnley, later playing for Bolton and in the States before finishing at Blackpool. These days golf is the centre of his sporting life.

Willie's undoubted ability gets him into the top 100, but it was a stormy time – and that's without mentioning a simmering rivalry between Willie and George Best!

Brian Kidd summed Morgan up well when he said: "Willie was a dribbler, a throw-back to the old-fashioned wingers."

> "I cannot think of a better player in his position in English football, nor in the world."
>
> TOMMY DOCHERTY

JACKIE BLANCHFLOWER

Jackie Blanchflower will be remembered not only for his stylish play for Manchester United and Northern Ireland, but for his bravery at the end of his life.

Although fighting a losing battle with illness, Jackie, who died in 1998 aged 65, refused to accept defeat until it was impossible for him to carry on any longer.

Only a fortnight before his death and already gravely ill, he insisted on attending the Munich Memorial Fund match at Old Trafford in order to meet up once again with his former teammates, especially fellow-survivors of the air disaster in 1958.

A month before that, he was still keeping his appointments as an after-dinner speaker. His last function was a sportsmen's night at Sandbach in Cheshire, where I am told he brought the house down and received a standing ovation. His ability to entertain was honed relatively late in his life and was his answer to a career wrecked by the injuries he received in the Munich tragedy. A badly-broken arm and, critically, a smashed pelvis ended his playing career at the age of 25, and again it was his remarkable spirit which over the years saw him win through a number of setbacks to make his mark as a brilliantly funny man, drawing not just on his experiences with Manchester United but on a natural Irish wit which was sharp and ironic.

Jean Blanchflower, his wife of 42 years, said at his funeral: "He had bookings through into next year, but right to the end as he lay in bed his thoughts were about how he didn't want to let anyone down. It was only with the greatest reluctance that he accepted he couldn't get up to Scotland just a few weeks before he died.

"'He was determined to get to the Munich match, though, despite being so very poorly. Maybe not everyone liked him as a footballer, but I never came across anyone who didn't like him as a person."

A Northern Ireland schoolboy international, he arrived at Old Trafford as a youngster to become one of the Busby Babes and in his early days he cleaned the boots of players like Charlie Mitten, but by the time he was 22 he had won a League championship medal.

He played as an emergency goalkeeper the following year in the 1957 FA Cup final against Aston Villa following injury to Ray Wood, but the next season he had to compete with Mark Jones for the centre-half position.

He played with his older brother, Danny, in a successful Northern Ireland team which reached the World Cup finals in Sweden in 1958.

He didn't play against Red Star in Belgrade but travelled as a reserve on the plane, which crashed trying to take off after the refuelling stop in Munich. Harry Gregg found him lying on the runway and used his tie to stop the bleeding from his mangled arm.

Harry, his saviour that day, was just one of the old players Jackie wanted to see again when he forced himself to attend the Munich Memorial match and perhaps thought of the even more unfortunate players like Tommy Taylor, best man at his wedding, who didn't come back at all.

"Maybe not everyone liked him as a footballer, but I never came across anyone who didn't like him as a person."

JEAN BLANCHFLOWER PAYING TRIBUTE TO HER HUSBAND AT HIS FUNERAL IN 1998

BILLY WHELAN

Bill Foulkes remembers that on the last fateful attempt to take off at Munich, Billy Whelan quietly let it be known that if the worst happened he was ready, and Bill is in no doubt about what his team-mate had in mind as the plane roared down the runway to disaster.

"Billy was a devout Roman Catholic and would have made a good priest," he says about a man all the players recognised and respected for his gentle nature, reserve and modesty.

In fact Matt Busby's only reservation about Liam Whelan the footballer was a lack of confidence which he felt was inhibiting his undoubted skills. At the time of the Munich air crash he had been dropped in favour of the emerging Bobby Charlton, who once wrote about his rival: "He was a beautiful ball-player and an accomplished reader of the game. I remember playing in a youth friendly match in Switzerland when the Brazilian team, who were in training there at the time, turned up to watch. We won 9–2 and Whelan scored five. The Brazilians thought he was a fantastic prospect."

Indeed he was, and confidence in his own ability would surely have come with experience, for he was only 22 when he was killed and already he had established himself as a rare talent after making an unusual debut.

Spotted by United's legendary Irish scout Billy Behan, he was signed from the Dublin club Home Farm and rushed into the final of the 1953 FA Youth Cup as a replacement for the injured John Doherty. He scored in each game of the two-leg final as United beat Wolves 7–1 at Old Trafford and drew 2–2 away.

To win a medal in his first game for a new club was special, but it set a pattern which saw him win Championship medals almost as quickly. He made his senior debut in 1955 and the next three years with the zestful Busby Babes saw him share in the League title successes of 1956 and 1957.

Goals became his hallmark, remarkably so for a scheming inside-forward whose main job was to create chances for others, and in a total of 96 League and Cup games he scored 52 goals. Early in season 1956–57 he set a record by scoring in eight successive League games on his way to a League total of 26 goals from 39 appearances to help win the title.

He was the top scorer as well as helping the team reach the final of the FA Cup and enjoy a sparkling first season in the European Cup.

It was the quarter-final 5–3 defeat against Bilbao in Spain that he picked out as his favourite memory of the season. Contributing to a brochure commemorating their great year in three competitions, Billy Whelan wrote: "Scoring the best goal of my life five minutes from time in Bilbao. It was the goal that put us back with a chance for the second leg."

United won the return 3–0 playing at Maine Road, and thanks to Whelan's goal took the tie 6–5 on aggregate to reach the semi-finals. They had made a lasting impact on Europe.

Whelan had been an inspiration, which made it all the more surprising when Matt Busby continued his revolution by putting more youngsters into the team at the expense of players like Whelan, not exactly an old-timer at 22.

Tragically for Whelan, he still went on the trip to Belgrade as a reserve, to lose his life before it had really begun.

"He was a beautiful ball-player and an accomplished reader of the game."
BOBBY CHARLTON

Joe Jordan had a name made for newspaper headlines, and he was variously described in his days at Old Trafford as "Smokin' Joe" or even "Snarling Joe".

Of course it was his style of play and aggression that lay behind the tough-guy labels, and in action – without his front teeth – he wasn't a pretty sight. In fact with his eye-teeth made prominent by the absence of the top row in between he looked to have fangs and, to be honest, he was a fearsome, frightening sight!

But what a charming contrast off the field. Put through Don Revie's finishing-school at Leeds, "Jaws" Jordan and Gordon McQueen were brought up to be media-friendly and both arrived at Old Trafford in the publicity-shy era of Dave Sexton like a breath of fresh air.

The barnstorming centre-forward is also very much a family man with four children, the two boys never letting him forget his days at Old Trafford.

"When the boys were young they were both committed Reds," he told me. "I think it was all down to Bryan Robson. We were on holiday and met him. He played football with them and when they got back home Bryan's pictures and photographs were plastered on their bedroom walls.

"Mind you, I didn't exactly discour-age them because I was a United fan long before I ever played for them. My father was as well, and that's because we come from the same village in Scotland as Jimmy Delaney.

"Jimmy played for United just after the war and he was a big name in our village. I think he was a friend of my dad's, and so naturally we all followed his career and became United supporters.

"It was a great experience when I eventually came to play at Old Trafford, and I think it also gave my father a lot of pleasure. I enjoyed all my clubs. Each one was a different chapter in my life. I was pretty fortunate and have no regrets about my transfers."

And what a marvellous playing pedigree he put together. His international record was outstanding. He won 52 caps and became the first Scot to score in three World Cup final tournaments.

He played for Leeds in their great days with Don Revie and in his eight years at Elland Road won a League Championship medal. Twice United's top scorer, he played in the 1979 FA Cup final in his three years at Old Trafford before sampling the high life abroad with AC Milan and Verona. He came home to play for Southampton and was still in action at the age of 37 as player-manager of Bristol City.

He had a spell as assistant manager of Northern Ireland with Laurie McMenemy and more recently has been Lou Macari's assistant at Huddersfield Town. Incidentally, one of his boys has since defected to Everton but Andrew is still a diehard United fan.

Not so long ago I watched Leeds United's old boys beat Manchester United's in a charity match at York, and one of the reasons for Leeds' success was – yes, Smokin' Joe, nearly 50 but still giving it everything.

PROFILE

BORN Carluke, Motherwell
DATE OF BIRTH 15 December 1951
JOINED UNITED January 1978
FEE £350,000
PREVIOUS CLUBS Morton, Leeds United
UNITED LEAGUE APPS 109
GOALS 37
INTERNATIONAL CAPS (Scotland) 52
GOALS 11

> "I enjoyed all my clubs. Each one was a different chapter in my life. I was pretty fortunate and have no regrets about my transfers."
>
> JOE JORDAN

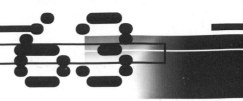

RAY WILKINS

Ron Atkinson has a lot to answer for when it comes to Ray Wilkins, for it was Big Ron when manager of Manchester United who labelled one of England's finest as "The Crab".

It was an attempt by the Reds' boss to jolt Ray out of his tendency to move the ball sideways, even backwards, rather than press forward in a more penetrating way. Nevertheless it was a harsh jibe at a player who was probably ahead of his time.

Never mind Martin Peters: Ray Wilkins, with his careful emphasis on keeping possession of the ball and changing angles of play, was merely giving United supporters a foretaste of the Eric Cantona era when moving the ball around regardless of yards gained became a better-understood tactic.

The remark obviously went home, though, as Ray later told me: "Ron Atkinson called me a crab, always going sideways, and it stuck. Everyone mentions it. I can in fact go forward like anyone, but it's only possible to play about fifty per cent of passes forward and most managers have wanted me to be a play-maker, which means working across the pitch as well as down it."

In any case the Wilkins style certainly didn't put many people off, as he plied his trade for Chelsea, Manchester United, AC Milan, Paris St Germain, Glasgow Rangers, Queen's Park Rangers, Crystal Palace, QPR again as player-manager, Wycombe Wanderers, Hibernian, Millwall and Leyton Orient. Some career for a crab, nearly 25 years of first-team football before a busy coaching and management career.

But then Wilkins was never really a Ron Atkinson man. It was Dave Sexton as manager at Stamford Bridge who gave the Londoner his chance, making him Chelsea's youngest-ever captain at 18, and it was Sexton of course who brought Wilkins to Old Trafford for an £825,000 fee in August 1979.

Although Wilkins went on to score a rare but lovely goal in the FA Cup final against Brighton to earn a replay and eventual victory, the new boss seemed intent on building his team round his own man, Bryan Robson. He took the captaincy off Wilkins in favour of Robson while the skipper was recovering from a broken cheekbone, and though he had just won the supporters' Player of the Year award, it was Atkinson who sold him to AC Milan for £1.5 million in summer 1984.

He thrived in Italy just as he did playing for England 84 times, remaining a master stylist throughout his career.

Michael Parkinson summed him up well in a TV interview saying that if football wanted to promote the game with the ideal image they would have to invent someone like Ray Wilkins. In 1993 he received the MBE for his services to football. Dave Sexton recalls: "I remember him coming along for training at Chelsea as a young schoolboy and instantly he was a player far more mature than his years. He was a thoroughbred who captained the England youth team and by the age of 17 he was ready for first-team football. I was manager by this time and had no hesitation in giving him his League debut in a London derby. He became our captain at 18 and by the time he was 19 he was playing for England. The great thing about him is that he took all his youthful success in his stride and did not let his early fame spoil his attitude to the game."

PROFILE

BORN Hillingdon, London
DATE OF BIRTH 14 September 1956
JOINED UNITED August 1979
FEE £825,000
PREVIOUS CLUB Chelsea
UNITED LEAGUE APPS 160
GOALS 7
INTERNATIONAL CAPS (England) 84
GOALS 3

"I remember him coming along for training at Chelsea as a young schoolboy and instantly he was a player far more mature than his years."
DAVE SEXTON, WILKINS' BOSS AT BOTH STAMFORD BRIDGE AND OLD TRAFFORD

GARY BAILEY

It's true he had been coached by his father, Roy Bailey of Ipswich Town fame, after his dad had upped sticks at the end of his playing career and headed for South Africa, taking his young family with him.

But keeping goal for Wits University in Johannesburg is not the usual springboard for First Division football in England. United only took him on trial, yet after just a few weeks he was catapulted into a League debut, and almost as quickly was playing for the England Under-21 team.

If ever there was such a thing as being born with a silver soccer spoon in your mouth, Gary Bailey was.

Yet, though it seemed he had started at the top, nobody could have worked harder to justify his position. All his managers would later testify to his dedication and willingness to work. He was conscientious beyond immediate football duty, too. Visiting hospitals, chatting to sponsors, meeting fans and signing autographs is not every player's favourite pastime, but Gary was always one of the most willing and cheerful.

At the end of his playing days, the chairman said he would miss him, and he wasn't just thinking about his goalkeeping!

Ironically his career came to an end almost as quickly as it had started, and long before his proper time. He had eight years at the top and then knee problems, which had started on international duty, forced him to quit at 28, especially young for a goalkeeper.

Although his career seemed to have been dropped in his lap, he had to fight hard along the way. A few of his fellow-professionals who had come up the hard way were a little suspicious and resentful of the young man from university, complete with a typical South African's self-belief and confidence.

They laughed at his attempt to install a flock of ducks. He had a pond created for them at the bottom of his garden in his new house in Didsbuy, only he forgot to have their wings clipped and they all flew off.

He bought a new lot and made sure they couldn't fly, which worked well until someone left the gate open and they all waddled off to the nearby river and swam to freedom.

Yes, they laughed; but nobody louder than Gary himself, who left a lot of friends when he went back to South Africa where he is now a major television sports star.

Ron Atkinson, his former manager at Old Trafford, said: "He always had this burning ambition to become the number one goalkeeper. At one point it had become such an obsession that it was inhibiting him. He was nearly paranoid and we had to teach him to relax a little and be patient. It's one thing to be ambitious but it doesn't help to get uptight about it."

There was always a touch of Roy of the Rovers about Gary Bailey with his blond hair, tall athletic physique, clean-cut good looks, South African tan and meteoric rise to the top.

PROFILE

BORN Ipswich
DATE OF BIRTH 9 August 1958
JOINED UNITED January 1978
FEE None
PREVIOUS CLUBS Kaiser Chiefs, Wits University
UNITED LEAGUE APPS 294
GOALS 0
INTERNATIONAL CAPS (England) 2
GOALS 0

"He always had this burning ambition to be the number one goalkeeper. At one point he was nearly paranoid and we had to teach him to relax a little and be patient. It's one thing to be ambitious but it doesn't help to get uptight about it."

RON ATKINSON

GORDON HILL

Gordon Hill went a long way towards making wingers popular again after Sir Alf Ramsey had won the World Cup with his "wingless wonders" of 1966.

With Gordon on the left and Steve Coppell racing up and down the right, Tommy Docherty had two penetrating wingers who were so successful they were picked for England.

Both were recruited from lower division clubs and reflected the Doc's canny eye for picking out players with unfulfilled potential.

Hill had a cracking finish and was scoring freely for Benny Fenton at Millwall when Docherty snapped him up for £70,000 plus what at the time seemed an improbable extra £10,000 if he played for England.

It was an inspired signing. In his 100 League starts for United he scored 39 goals. Goal-hanging poachers would be pleased with that kind of scoring rate, but to do it from the wing in addition to supplying a lot of crosses was marvellously exciting.

In Cup football Hill had an even better return of 10 goals from 24 outings in the two domestic competitions. Two of his most dramatic came in the 1976 FA Cup semi-final against Derby County at Hillsborough in a 2–0 win.

'I remember Leighton James in conversation before the match and Charlie George turning round to say it was not worth our lot bothering to turn up," he recalled. "I reminded them about that after we had won. We lost the final that season, but won the Cup the next year against Liverpool, and if Tommy Docherty had stayed I think we would have gone on to win the Championship."

Stuart Pearson, who relished his crosses, says, "Gordon is one of the best goalscoring wingers England has ever produced."

Not everyone saw Gordon Hill as a hero. Captain Martin Buchan cuffed him round the ear during a game because he considered the winger was neglecting his defensive duties.

"Everyone asks me about that,' says Gordon. 'The thing is that I can't defend to save my life, unlike Steve Coppell who used to go up and down all day. But maybe if I had defended more I wouldn't have scored my goals.

"Martin was a perfectionist. I didn't exactly love him but I enjoyed playing in the same team. The incident came really from frustration, though after he had hit me in front of everyone I told him that if he did it again I would kick him up in the air, or words to that effect. The referee said: 'Don't do that, because I've never sent two players off from the same team before.'"

After United, he had a brief spell with Derby and then linked up again with Tommy Docherty at Queen's Park Rangers.

He spent five years in the States developing his coaching skills, and played in Holland before returning to the Manchester area to work with Stuart Pearson at Northwich Victoria and then become player-manager of Stafford before his recent appointment as director of football at Chester.

"Once you have played for Manchester United you are never forgotten and I have lovely memories and friends here," he explained.

> "Once you have played for
> Manchester United you are never
> forgotten and I have lovely
> memories and friends here."
> GORDON HILL

PROFILE

BORN Sunbury-on-Thames
DATE OF BIRTH 1 April 1954
JOINED UNITED November 1975
FEE £80,000
PREVIOUS CLUBS Staines, Slough, Southall, Millwall, Chicago Sting (loan)
UNITED LEAGUE APPS 101
GOALS 39
INTERNATIONAL CAPS 6
GOALS 0

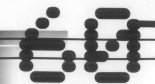

ALLENBY CHILTON

Sir Matt Busby had a fondness for attacking players dusted with magic, but there was one position where he consistently fielded men of a different make-up.

Busby liked a strong, commanding figure at centre-half, and after switching Allenby Chilton from wing-half to the middle of the defence the strapping six-footer, who had been training as a boxer, set the benchmark at number five for Manchester United.

He was a classical stopper who so impressed Busby that he went on selecting the same kind of defender throughout his career, with Mark Jones and latterly Bill Foulkes both exponents of the art of rugged defending.

So though Allenby Chilton did not attract a great deal of comment during his playing career, his influence was far-reaching and he was certainly the foundation of the new manager's successful post-war team.

Chilton arrived at Old Trafford before the war, signed by Scott Duncan from Seaham Colliery in the North-East and making his debut against Charlton Athletic the day before war was declared in September 1939.

He joined the Durham Light Infantry and was twice wounded in the fighting which followed the D-Day landings in Normandy.

Before that he had played for a number of clubs in wartime football, notably Cardiff, Newcastle and Charlton, where he helped to win the League Cup South.

He was 28 before he was able to resume his United career, but that did not stop him playing for a further 10 years, with Busby maintaining that he got better as he got older.

A pillar of strength in the 1948 FA Cup final victory which gave Busby his first trophy, he was not mentioned much in the reports because he was not that kind of player.

Effectiveness was his quality, the archetypal strong, silent type who was always there, rarely injured.

He went on to share in the 1952 Championship success as an ever-present, and proved the most durable of the post-war team, playing in almost 400 League and Cup games.

Taking over as captain from Johnny Carey, he held his place long enough to play alongside the Busby Babes, and when he finally gave way to Mark Jones, in February 1955, Chilton had achieved a club record of 166 consecutive League appearances.

The fact that Chilton played only twice for England was probably a reflection of his lack of a showy style rather than his talent because, as his old team-mates will tell you, there was no better centre-half around in that era.

He left United to become player-manager of Grimsby Town and lead them to the Third Division North Championship. He then had spells in management with Wigan and Hartlepool before settling in the Hull area, where he died in 1996.

PROFILE

BORN Sunderland
DATE OF BIRTH 16 September 1918
JOINED UNITED November 1938
FEE None
PREVIOUS CLUBS Liverpool (amateur), Seaham Colliery
UNITED LEAGUE APPS 353
GOALS 3

"Though he did not attract a great deal of comment during his playing career, his influence was far-reaching and he was certainly the foundation of the new manager's successful post-war team. Effectiveness was his quality, the archetypal strong, silent type who was always there."

JACK ROWLEY

Jack Rowley was an anti-tank gunner for six and a half years with the South Staffordshire infantry during the Second World War, but his nickname of "Gunner" had much more to do with his shooting on the football field.

The United and England centre forward, who died in 1998, was renowned for his ferocity and accuracy in striking a ball, both on the ground and in the air, which netted him 208 goals in 422 League and FA Cup appearances despite his long break from the game as a soldier.

Not that he stopped scoring during the war when he guested for Spurs, Wolves and Distillery among other clubs. Indeed, he always claimed that it was war-time football which provided him with one of his most cherished memories.

"I played for Spurs one week and scored seven, and then a few days later I got eight out of eight for Wolves," he once told me.

United fans, of course, will remember him for deeds closer to home, such as his two goals in the FA Cup final victory over Blackpool in 1948 and the 30 League goals he scored in season 1951–52 to break the club scoring record and secure Sir Matt Busby's first Championship success.

He dominated United's scoring in the early post-war years when he allied his fierce finishing with an equally strong and aggressive style of play. His robust style perhaps explains why in his later years he was more likely to be seen at his local rugby clubs. "I like the way rugby players take the knocks, shake them off and then later are the best of pals in the bar," he used to say.

He was certainly regarded by his team-mates as a strong-willed, forceful character, at times even a little awkward, and he was always willing to look

Busby in the eye.

These were perhaps the qualities which also brought him some success in management, after a career with United which spanned 18 years. He joined Plymouth as player-manager, eventually bringing them into the Second Division. Six months later he was sacked, possibly because his management style was a little like his play – aggressive and blunt.

However, this did not prevent him enjoying great success at Oldham, where in three years he won promotion and lifted the average attendance from 4,000 to 15,000.

He was one of the early English managers to be head-hunted by a leading European club, and he took Ajax into second place in the Dutch League before returning home for spells with Wrexham, Bradford and a second stint at Oldham, which suited him because he still had his Post Office and newsagent's shop at nearby Shaw from his earlier time in Lancashire.

Born in Wolverhampton, his father was a goalkeeper with Walsall who was still playing inside-forward for a local team when he was nearly 60. His youngest brother, Arthur, played for Leicester and became a scoring hero for Shrewsbury Town where he set any number of scoring records.

Jack started as part of Major Frank Buckley's nursery at Wolves. He didn't impress and was allowed to join Bournemouth, but after scoring 10 goals in 11 games Scott Duncan brought him aged 18 to Old Trafford for £3,000.

"I played for Spurs one week and scored seven, and then a few days later I got eight out of eight for Wolves."

JACK ROWLEY RELIVING HIS SUCCESSES IN WARTIME FOOTBALL

PROFILE

BORN Wolverhampton
DATE OF BIRTH 7 October 1920
JOINED UNITED October 1937
FEE £3,000
PREVIOUS CLUBS Wolves, Bournemouth
UNITED LEAGUE APPS 380
GOALS 182
INTERNATIONAL CAPS (England) 6
GOALS 6

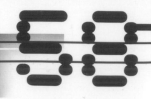

JIMMY GREENHOFF

"People have been kind enough to say that I was the best footballer never to win a full cap."

JIMMY GREENHOFF
ON MISSING OUT
ON ENGLAND
GLORY

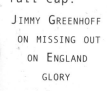

Manchester United, with their Busby Babe and Fergie Fledgling youth image, don't often sign 30-year-old players, but Tommy Docherty was more than happy to make an exception for Jimmy Greenhoff.

The Doc wanted to boost his firepower with a high-scoring partner for Stuart Pearson after moving Lou Macari to a slightly deeper role and, after noting his consistent marksmanship in his seven years at Stoke, paid £100,000 to bring him to Old Trafford in November 1976.

The move came as a complete surprise to the player, who thought that at the age of 30 he would be in the Potteries for the rest of his career.

"Having helped to win the League Cup in 1972 and then going close to the League title in 1975, I hadn't dreamed of leaving," he said, "but then one of the Victoria Ground stands blew down and money was desperately needed. The manager, Tony Waddington, pulled me to one side and told me, with tears in his eyes, that a bid had come in for me and someone had to go. I was dumbfounded, and if it hadn't been United I would have dug my heels in and stayed."

The Doc described him as the last piece in the jigsaw after returning to the First Division and his one-touch style fitted in perfectly with the quicksilver Pearson.

Jimmy is critical of his time at Old Trafford, suggesting that he should have been more selfish and gone for goal himself instead of playing the support role as much as he did. That way he might have won more at international level than an appearance for the England Under-23 team as an over-age player!

He says now: "People have been kind enough to say that I was the best footballer never to win a full cap, and it's lovely to hear, but in all honesty I would rather have had a cap than the tribute."

There were compensations, though, as he teamed up with his brother Brian, a United player since he was a youngster, and in Jimmy's first full season they appeared together in the team which beat Liverpool 2–1 to carry home the 1977 FA Cup.

Jimmy was credited with the winning goal but he confesses: "Lou Macari's shot hit me on the chest and skewed into goal. I thought: 'Thank you very much; I'll take that!'"

Later he played alongside Joe Jordan up front and won the supporters' Player of the Year award, and says: "I treasure it more than any other honour. Sometimes retired footballers have to sell their memorabilia to help them through bad times, but if I was in that situation, my trophy from the fans would be the last to go."

He was 34 when he left United to play for Crewe, Toronto Blizzard and then Port Vale before becoming player-manager at Rochdale.

He had an unhappy financial experience in the insurance business when his partner was convicted of fraud, but he pulled through and works in the Potteries where he has always lived.

"I can't separate United and Stoke in my affections. I had fantastic times with both clubs and I will always love them both," he says.

KEVIN MORAN

It may be said in boxing that a particular fighter cuts easily, but the expression also applied to football when Kevin Moran was in action.

The United defender always seemed to be in the wars, with gashes on his head and his face. The tabloid papers soon dubbed him Captain Blood and he eventually totalled a hundred stitches.

It wasn't a matter of tender skin, either. Kevin got his cuts and bruises the hard way, heading opposing centre forward's heads and generally putting his head in danger areas with no fear for the consequences.

You have only to glance at his early days as a sportsman to discover where he acquired his cavalier approach to injuries – for Gaelic football was the name of the game which occupied the youthful Irishman growing up in Dublin. In fact he was rather good at it, and played in three All-Ireland finals in three years.

But Billy Behan, United's veteran scout in Dublin who had sent people like Billy Whelan, Johnny Giles and Tony Dunne across to England, spotted Moran playing a few games for Pegasus, his university team.

Kevin explained: "I had no thought of playing professional soccer in England. I was set for a career in chartered accountancy, and when Billy asked me to go over for a trial I thought nothing would come of it. For that reason, I was totally relaxed, only stayed a few days and played in one friendly, but Dave Sexton, the manager, offered me terms to give me the hardest decision of my life. It took me the best part of a fortnight to make up my mind.

"In one way I didn't think I would make the grade in soccer and I was reluctant to give up the Gaelic at my peak. I decided, though, that if I didn't go I would probably regret it for the rest of my life."

Dave Sexton said: "This was a discovery in the real meaning of the word because as far as soccer was concerned he had not attracted a lot of attention. Billy Behan found him and convinced everyone he had great potential at our game."

The player's love of the Gaelic game was so strong that Sexton at first allowed him to play both sports. He went back home in the summer of 1978 to compete for his third final, only to report back to Old Trafford with a ripped hamstring and eight stitches in his forehead.

That was the end of his Gaelic career, but soon there was ample compensation as he took over from Gordon McQueen to play for three managers at Old Trafford and appear in two FA Cup-winning teams.

He certainly won't forget the second one against Everton, when he became the first player to be sent off in the Wembley showpiece.

Sir Alex Ferguson let him join Sporting Gijon in Northern Spain but after 18 months abroad he returned to play for Blackburn Rovers for nearly five years to take him to the age of 38 and extend his international career with the Republic to 71 caps.

As tough as they come, durable, a player who gave his all and is still linked with Old Trafford as a committee member of the Association of Former Manchester United Players, he was chairman in the year 2000 and works with Pro-Active Sports Management representing players and in their hospitality division.

PROFILE

BORN Dublin
DATE OF BIRTH 29 April 1956
JOINED UNITED February 1978
FEE None
PREVIOUS CLUB Pegasus, Dublin University
UNITED LEAGUE APPS 231
GOALS 31
INTERNATIONAL CAPS (Republic of Ireland) 71

"When Billy Behan asked me to go for a trial I thought nothing would come of it. But Dave Sexton [gave] me the hardest decision of my life."

KEVIN MORAN ON COMING TO UNITED

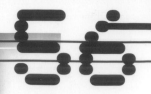

SHAY BRENNAN

Shay Brennan always used to claim that he made the goal that won the European Cup for Manchester United in 1968.

He would acknowledge that George Best was the scorer two minutes into extra time, and if pushed would concede that it wasn't a bad goal. In fact it was brilliant, but Shay preferred to dwell on the build-up with tongue firmly in his cheek. "I got this ball and knocked it back to our goalkeeper. Alex Stepney kicked it down the field, Brian Kidd headed it on and Bestie raced away to score. But I started the move and if I hadn't laid back that pass to Alex Stepney we wouldn't have scored… would we?" he used to ask with a big grin, and you just had to agree!

That was Shay Brennan, a man with a bubbling, infectious sense of humour, and as former Busby Babe John Doherty, says: "In the dressing-room and among the players, I think Shay Brennan was the most popular player United ever had. Everybody liked him."

His popularity behind the scenes perhaps went unnoticed by the public because he was a modest man who did his best to avoid publicity, but could do little to keep himself out of the headlines when he came into United's first team because he was major news.

It was in the dark days after Munich when, from being a junior in the reserves, he was suddenly thrust into the senior side as Jimmy Murphy desperately put a team together to replace the side wiped out in the disaster.

Shay, a forward in the team which won the FA Youth Cup in 1955, was at outside-left in the patched-up side which met Sheffield Wednesday in the fifth round of the FA Cup at Old Trafford, their first game after the crash.

He scored twice in a remarkable 3–0 win and naturally stayed in the team for his League debut against Nottingham Forest three days later.

Although he lost his place for the FA Cup final at the end of the season as more senior players recovered from their injuries to play again, he won two League championship medals and shared in the historic European Cup final victory against Benfica in 1968.

In all he made over 360 first-team appearances for United and won 19 caps for the Republic of Ireland.

He was always happy to play a supporting role from his right-back position, accepting there were players in the team better fitted to create the magic. Every team needs a player or two like that to knit the superstars together and make them twinkle.

Later he became player-manager of Waterford in the Republic of Ireland and settled in nearby Tremore where he ran a parcel courier business. He suffered a heart attack in 1986 and successfully came through a heart by-pass operation, but died suddenly on Wexford Golf Course at the age of 63 in June 2000.

PROFILE

BORN Manchester
DATE OF BIRTH 6 May 1937
JOINED UNITED April 1955
FEE None
PREVIOUS CLUB Junior
UNITED LEAGUE APPS 292
GOALS 3
INTERNATIONAL CAPS (Republic of Ireland) 19
GOALS 0

> "In the dressing-room and among the players, I think Shay Brennan was the most popular player United ever had. Everybody liked him."
> BUSBY BABE JOHN DOHERTY

ARTHUR ALBISTON

Arthur Albiston served Manchester United in the way of many Old Trafford left backs like Tony Dunne and Denis Irwin: no fuss, no frills, loyal and most effective for a decade or more.

His well-deserved testimonial against Manchester City was a fitting finale because it was against City that he originally had a taste of the first team, coming on as a young substitute in Tony Dunne's testimonial in 1973 before his competitive debut a year later against the Blues in the League Cup.

The most dramatic moment in his early days, though, was his first appearance in the FA Cup final. Stewart Houston damaged his ankle shortly before the big day to bring in 19-year-old Albiston for a Cup debut against Liverpool in the 1977 final. He played impressively in a 2–1 win to justify the faith of Tommy Docherty, and sportingly offered his winner's medal to the luckless Houston. It was graciously refused, but it was a sincere gesture by the always fair-minded Scot.

The following season he became a regular making nearly 500 appearances in all competitions and becoming the first United player to win three FA Cup winners' medals.

Europe also figures prominently in his memories, especially a semi–final against Juventus in the Cup Winners' Cup of season 1983–84 when he and Mike Duxbury were the full-backs.

Ron Atkinson's team came close to winning through to the final against the Italian giants after drawing the first leg 1–1 at Old Trafford. Recalls Arthur: "The manager proved himself an uncanny forecaster of tactics and how Juventus would play in the return. In the team talk he told us to be aware of Platini and his ability to spray long, accurate passes to set people attacking. Then he said we had to watch out for Boniek, the Polish striker, who he said was very good at getting on to the end of Platini's passes to run at goal.

"Blow me, the game wasn't very old when Platini flung a great pass forward on my side of the field for Boniek to break between Graeme Hogg and myself. He went straight for goal, shot, and Juventus were a goal up. I thought, 'Thanks for warning us, Ron, but you might have explained how to stop them as well!'"

Later in his career Albiston lost his regular place but Sir Alex Ferguson, his third manager, did not hesitate to say: "Arthur has not had much of a chance since his injury, but that kind of thing happens to the best of players and even though he has not been in the actual team, he has always been interested and alert when we have had our squad talks. He is a marvellous professional, solid gold, and I often hold him up as the model for the young players to aim for."

Such was his level of fitness that after Old Trafford he played for one of his former managers, Ron Atkinson, at West Bromwich and then went on to Dundee, Chesterfield, Chester and Norwegian team Molde.

Nowadays, still living in the area, he is a regular in the Old Trafford press box as a radio commentator and analyst.

Arthur has always maintained his links with the club, working with the boys at United's school of excellence.

PROFILE

BORN Edinburgh
DATE OF BIRTH 14 July 1957
JOINED UNITED July 1972
FEE None
PREVIOUS CLUB Junior
UNITED LEAGUE APPS 379
GOALS 6
INTERNATIONAL CAPS (Scotland) 14
GOALS 0

"He is a marvellous professional, solid gold, and I often hold him up as the model for the young players."
SIR ALEX FERGUSON

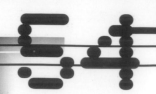

GORDON STRACHAN

Manchester United have Ron Atkinson to thank for bringing Gordon Strachan to Old Trafford, whipping him from under the noses of Cologne for a fee of £600,000 from Aberdeen.

He had a great track record at Pittodrie where he was part of Alex Ferguson's team which broke the monopoly of the Glasgow giants to collect two Scottish Premier League championship titles, three Scottish FA Cup winners' medals and the European Cup Winners' Cup of 1983.

He didn't disappoint in England, delighting the fans with his throw-back style of play which was in keeping with Scotland's tradition of producing "tanner ball players".

Like everyone else in the Atkinson era he missed out on an English League title, but he was a regular visitor to Wembley for various cup finals and was in a team which was always at least challenging for the Championship.

He must have thought life had turned in a mysterious circle when Big Ron's departure brought his old Aberdeen boss in as his successor in November 1986. We all wanted to know what the new manager was like and whether he really did throw cups and saucers at players in the dressing room when he wasn't best pleased.

"Wait and see," was the reply from Gordon with a sly grin, while inside he must have wondered what was in store for himself after a fairly stormy relationship with "Fiery Fergie".

In fact the transfer worked well for a couple of seasons, with Strachan saying: "Things are better now. Either the manager has mellowed or I have learned to keep out of the way better!"

However, a one-goal defeat at home against Nottingham Forest in the sixth round of the FA Cup, in March 1989, brought Gordon's days at United to an end, a parting of the ways which later had Sir Alex saying: "I am sure there are plenty of people who would argue that Strachan's transfer to Leeds United was the biggest mistake of my career.

"Certainly wee Gordon had the last laugh when Leeds pipped us for the Championship after he had become a key figure at Elland Road. But allowing Gordon to move on was the right thing to do. He had run out of steam for Manchester United. Compared to the player I knew of old he was only a shadow of his former self.

"I take nothing away from what he achieved at Leeds. He is a credit to himself with the way he looked after his fitness and he is a fine example to all young professionals, but he had no more to offer us. He needed a jolt and it triggered him back to life and the kind of form he had not shown in Manchester for a long time."

Gordon Strachan prospered after the £300,000 transfer and, always brighter than most, slipped naturally into management in 1995 as player-manager at Coventry, later retiring as a player to concentrate on the Sky Blues' annual relegation battle, before taking them down last season.

PROFILE

BORN Edinburgh
DATE OF BIRTH 9 February 1957
JOINED UNITED August 1984
FEE £600,000
PREVIOUS CLUBS Dundee, Aberdeen
UNITED LEAGUE APPS 160
GOALS 33
INTERNATIONAL CAPS (Scotland) 50
GOALS 5

"Allowing Gordon to move on was the right thing to do. He had run out of steam for Manchester United... He needed a jolt and it triggered him back to life and the kind of form he had not shown in Manchester for a long time."
SIR ALEX FERGUSON EXPLAINING HIS DECISION TO LET GORDON STRACHAN GO TO LEEDS UNITED

PHIL NEVILLE

It has always been said that blood is thicker than water, and if you ever needed proof in football, you just have to look at the brothers Neville of Manchester United.

They probably wouldn't understand if you talked to them about sibling rivalry because Gary and Philip are brothers who genuinely like each other and have grown up happy to spend time in each other's company.

They have football and playing for Manchester United in common, of course, but often they are competing head-to-head for a place in United's defence.

Philip, who like his older brother, arrived at Old Trafford from Bury schools football, says: "I enjoy being on the pitch with Gary and he is brilliant to play with. It's true we are competing for places, but we don't really see it that way. We are the best of friends. Some people, even at the club, think our being pals is a bit of an act but it is genuine. We have always stuck up for each other."

The brothers are also close to their sister Tracy, who is herself an England netball star. "We are pretty supportive," Phil explained. "When she was at university we always tried to look after her because students don't get a lot. Gary used to buy her loads of clothes and we tried to see she didn't go short.

"When possible we always tried to watch her netball internationals because we feel her achievement has been greater than ours. When she got into the squad she was only 19, the youngest by five or six years."

The intense competition for places at United has often left Phil Neville on the substitutes' bench, sparking off inquiries from other clubs.

"People would come up to me and ask if I was leaving, but the stories were laughable. The Boss was fine and wanting to leave has never entered my head. There is so much talent at this club, with around 20 full internationals, that you just don't expect to play every game. It wouldn't be realistic, and just to get selected as a substitute is an achievement in itself.

"You also have to bear in mind that playing 25 games for Manchester United is better than 40 for some other club. I am often on the bench, but just to be part of the build-up is fantastic."

Philip, who turned down the chance to become a professional cricketer in order to pursue his football career, has a similar pragmatic attitude towards playing for England. He was undoubtedly hurt when he was left out of the World Cup squad for France in 1998 after being in the original, slightly bigger party, and hurt when he wasn't selected for a friendly against Czechoslovakia after Glenn Hoddle had said he would be picking young players. But Sven-Göran Eriksson, the latest England manager, has included him in his squads and Phil says: "It's a bonus and honour to get an international selection but if I am playing well for Manchester United it will come anyway, so what I must do in the first instance is concentrate on my game for my club."

Phil has particularly enjoyed his international football this summer. With brother Gary injured, he took over the right-back position in a winning run which saw England successfully secure the points in their World Cup qualifier against Greece in Athens. The future looks good for Phil Neville.

PROFILE

BORN Bury
DATE OF BIRTH 21 January 1977
JOINED UNITED July 1993
FEE None
PREVIOUS CLUB Junior
UNITED LEAGUE APPS 160
GOALS 2
INTERNATIONAL CAPS (England) 33
GOALS 0

"Playing 25 games for Manchester United is better than 40 for some other clubs."

PHIL NEVILLE

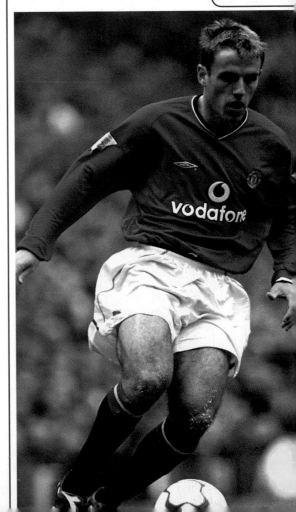

LEE SHARPE

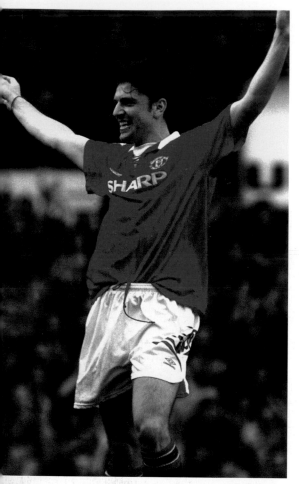

At the peak of his powers, Lee Sharpe was a compelling left-winger, and it was sad that for various reasons he did not stay the course at Old Trafford.

> "Lee Sharpe was something of a golden boy, but unlike the young stars following him, he did not seem able to sustain his commitment to the game, at least not in the eyes of his manager, who worried about his social life."

Sir Alex Ferguson got him from Torquay United at the age of 17 but by 25 he was on his way to Leeds and a roller-coaster career which did not really fulfil the promise of his exciting early achievements.

His finest years were undoubtedly at Old Trafford, where he helped Sir Alex Ferguson turn the corner and launch his assault on the game's top honours.

The United manager, tipped off by an old journalist friend who had retired to the south coast, was monitoring the progress of Sharpe at Torquay when he suddenly got word that the youngster had started to play in the first team.

Knowing this would alert rivals, he dashed to the holiday resort town and kept Cyril Knowles up half the night in order to make sure of the boy's transfer for £180,000. Sharpe was given his debut three months later, still only aged 17, and introduced as a left-back where his speed of recovery was notable and

where it was felt he would better learn his trade.

But over the next two seasons he developed as a winger with an ability to cross the ball at pace which made him so dramatic to watch and so effective for the team.

He helped win the European Cup Winners' Cup in 1991, and one of his most notable achievements came the same season when he took Highbury by storm and scored a hat-trick in a 6–2 victory over Arsenal in the fourth round of the Rumbelows Cup. He was on fire that night and scored a couple more goals in the competition on the way to the final and a narrow one-goal defeat against Sheffield Wednesday. He was voted the PFA Young Player of the Year and won the first of eight England caps.

Sharpe went on to help bring the League title back to Old Trafford in 1993 after a 26-year absence and shared in the League and FA Cup double the following year.

By now he was something of a golden boy, the forerunner of the new wave represented by Giggs and Beckham, but unlike the young stars following him he did not seem able to sustain his commitment to the game, at least not in the eyes of his manager, who worried about his social life.

Injuries and illness certainly did not help him towards the end of his time with United. The whole club were worried when he contracted viral meningitis. Although not the most virulent strain of the illness, it nevertheless cost him four months out of the game.

With Giggs now established on the left wing, Sharpe was sold to Leeds for £4.5 million, a handsome profit. He later played for David Platt in Italy with Sampdoria before returning home to join Bradford City and play on loan at Portsmouth.

PROFILE

BORN Halesowen
DATE OF BIRTH 27 May 1971
JOINED UNITED June 1988
FEE £180,000
PREVIOUS CLUB Torquay United
UNITED LEAGUE APPS 160
GOALS 33
INTERNATIONAL CAPS 8
GOALS 0

DAVID SADLER

Such was the athleticism and intelligence of David Sadler that he was equally comfortable playing in either attack or defence – or indeed anywhere in between!

Allied to an equable temperament and loyalty to his club, he took his shifting positions without complaint to prove himself a truly versatile player. Even so, one wonders whether he might have achieved even more than his four full England caps had he specialised in the defensive centre-back role which did not become his regular position until relatively late in his career.

He first came to the fore as a centre-forward with his local side, Maidstone United, when he was so outstanding that he played for the England amateur team at the age of 16.

He was a much sought after youngster and Matt Busby turned on all his charm to bring him to Old Trafford, where he played as an amateur for his first three months. Still a forward, he scored a hat-trick in the final of the FA Youth Cup against Swindon in a team which also featured George Best, his fellow-lodger in digs with Mrs Fullaway in Chorlton-cum-Hardy.

He soon made his first-team debut, replacing David Herd for a spell and then filling in for other forwards, with the result that he made 19 League appearances and scored five goals in his first full season of 1963–64.

He had a quiet couple of years, but then, with the help of the versatility which had seen him fill a number of different roles, he became an integral part of the team which won the 1967 Championship and the European Cup the following year.

As a forward, at first he didn't like the idea of playing in midfield and defence, but as he explained at the time: "I didn't want to become a 'basher' which playing centre-half can sometimes make you, but at the same time I wasn't unduly worried, because at least I was playing in the first team.

"I became a Jack-of-all trades, and in our League Championship success I played in three different positions. The following season saw me in five different shirt numbers."

Eventually, after an injury to Nobby Stiles, he settled into what he describes as his best position, playing as the defensive wing-half in the back four. He played right through the successful European Cup campaign of 1968, and it was his versatility which undoubtedly got them through to the final.

He was an ever-present in the European campaign but with his amazing adaptability he stood in at different times for Bill Foulkes, Nobby Stiles and Denis Law as they went through to beat Benfica 4–1 in the final at Wembley.

Looking back, he says now: "There is something very special about belonging to the élite 11 Manchester United players who won the European Cup all those years ago, but it is time to hand some of the European glory from the days of Sir Matt Busby over to Alex Ferguson's team."

After Old Trafford David played at Preston for four years, but his links with United run deep as the founding secretary of the Association of Former Manchester United Players – a job he still accomplishes with all his old versatility!

Outside football, he has his own company, David Sadler Promotions, after a period as a building society manager.

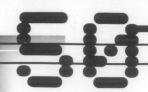

WES BROWN

Wes Brown is the answer to those who wondered whether Sir Alex Ferguson could carry on producing good young players following the success of his class of '92 which emerged to make up half the team for both United and England.

PROFILE

BORN Manchester
DATE OF BIRTH 13 October 1979
JOINED UNITED July 1996
FEE None
PREVIOUS CLUB Junior
UNITED LEAGUE APPS 44
GOALS 0
INTERNATIONAL CAPS (England) 3
GOALS 0

> "Wes Brown has been a sensation and is the best young centre-half I have ever seen."
>
> SIR ALEX FERGUSON

The centre-back department was still packed with experienced players when Steve Bruce and Gary Pallister relinquished their hold, but there was no denying the challenge of Wes Brown. Injuries perhaps opened the door, but the United manager had no hesitation after giving him his head.

"Wes Brown has been a sensation and is the best young centre-half I have ever seen," he said. "He has forced his way into the team despite fierce competition, a remarkable achievement after suffering a cruciate injury which kept him out of football for the best part of a year."

The ruptured tendon, a freak training-ground accident, saw him miss the whole of the 1999–2000 season and throw a shadow over an exceptional start which began at senior level with a debut at Barnsley on the last day of the 1997–98 season. The 18-year-old Manchester boy won a testing duel with the no-nonsense Ashley Ward.

He had made his mark, and next season made 21 first-team appearances to help land the unique treble, as well as winning an England debut at senior level under Kevin Keegan after making only 11 Premiership appearances.

He oozed defensive class; cool, and with time seemingly always on his side, however tight the situation. Then his world turned upside-down with the knee injury which saw him undergo the same operation as Roy Keane, Ben Thornley and Terry Cooke.

United wisely refused to rush him and he returned for the start of the 2000–01 season looking as good as ever, and at just the right time to help cover for the injured Jaap Stam.

His coach at United, Steve McClaren, summed up: "When Stam was injured and out for most of the first half of the season, Wes saw us through.

"He helped us over a difficult period. He is one of the most naturally-gifted players I have ever seen. I can see him as an England international for the next 10 years. People ask who can fill Tony Adams' shoes now he has gone. Well, Wes can! Young defenders usually make mistakes early on and then get better as they get older. If that's the case, who knows how good he is going to be?"

Says Brown: "When I got my injury it was gutting to be told how long I would be out. I was down for a few weeks, but I had to look on the bright side. You... think people are going to forget you, but the manager kept checking on my progress and encouraging me... I just concentrated on regaining my fitness. I thought about the players who had recovered, not the ones who hadn't."

Injury stopped him touring this summer, but Sven-Göran Eriksson has already indicated he is in his international plans with England.

JOHNNY BERRY

Johnny Berry suffered grievously in the Munich air crash with head injuries which not only ended his playing career but also left him with a legacy that in all probability shortened his life, and certainly damaged the quality of it.

He was a popular member of the Busby Babes team, despite being a "bought" player asked to fit in with the new-look youthful side being introduced when he was signed from Birmingham City for £27,000 in 1951.

Known affectionately by team-mates as "Digger", though small, his style was to dig in hard for the ball and race down the right wing. Matt Busby signed him to replace Jimmy Delaney, remembering, as he put it at the time, that in their clashes with Birmingham, Berry had led them a "merry dance".

He certainly justified this faith, and though his debut against Bolton was marked by a defeat he made the position his own for the next seven years. He was in the team which won the championship in 1952 and successfully adapted to the new side Busby was building. Though surrounded by an ever-growing band of younger men, he was a key man on the team which won the 1956 and 1957 Championships.

England picked up on him too, and after being capped at B level he won four full caps. Europe suited his pace and penetration on the wing, and he had a fierce shot for his 5ft 5in size, with a good scoring return for a winger of 37 League goals in 247 appearances.

Most players of his era found the war upset their careers, but Berry might have missed out on professional football had it not been for service with the Royal Artillery. He impressed Fred Harris, a fellow-soldier who was also captain of Birmingham City, and he was invited to St Andrews for a trial that saw him taken on at the age of 20. He was with Birmingham for seven years and made over a hundred League appearances before moving to Old Trafford.

Ironically, just before Munich he lost his place to Kenny Morgans and didn't play in the last League game at Arsenal, nor the second leg of the fateful European Cup quarter-final in Belgrade, but was in the squad – and the aircraft.

Johnny spent the rest of the season in hospital, returning the next season but with no chance of playing again. The club helped with his rehabilitation, but eventually he returned to his home town of Aldershot where he went into business in a sports shop with his brother Peter, who had played for Crystal Palace and Peterborough.

He later worked in a television parts warehouse, but sadly the crash left him a changed man until his death in 1994.

PROFILE

BORN Aldershot
DATE OF BIRTH 1 June 1926
JOINED UNITED August 1951
FEE £27,000
PREVIOUS CLUB Birmingham City
UNITED LEAGUE APPS 247
GOALS 37
INTERNATIONAL CAPS (England) 4
GOALS 0

"Known affectionately as 'Digger', though small, his style was to dig in hard for the ball and race down the right wing."

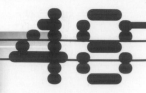

JOHNNY CAREY

He was always known as "Gentleman John": easy-going, pipe-smoking and quite imperturbable. Nothing ever seemed to bother him, either on or off the field.

Johnny Carey was a highly-influential player, too, and if the readership of the magazine who voted for the greatest players had included more older supporters, he would have figured a lot higher in the list!

In his era, spanning the Second World War, he was held in such esteem that at the end of his 17 years at Old Trafford he was invited by the directors to the boardroom so they could express their appreciation. The minutes recorded: "By his outstanding personality as a true sportsman, the honours he had won as an international in club matches, he had covered his career with glory and set a shining example to all who follow him."

Carey would have taken even this tribute in his stride because, as John Doherty, a Busby Babe who made his debut when Carey was captain, recalled: "I can't recollect him ever getting annoyed, not even if someone had kicked him. He seemed to stroll through games. If he was playing today he would be called laid-back. Then we just thought he was unflappable.

"He was a great player, and as a captain his influence was immense. He was a thinker, but not a shouter."

Carey arrived at Old Trafford in 1936 almost by accident. Chief scout Louis Rocca had gone to Dublin to sign a player who changed his mind. So as not to waste the journey, Rocca went to watch St James's Gate play and recalled: "It was a poor game but there was something about the inside right which took my fancy. A meeting of the committee was called there and then. We talked for hours and eventually I got Carey's signature for £200."

Not even Rocca could have imagined 17-year-old Carey would become a giant so versatile he figured in 10 different positions, including goal after Jack Crompton had been taken ill on an away trip. Rocca concluded: "No greater Irish player crossed the Channel to make a name in English football."

He played for two seasons before war was declared and he joined the Queen's Royal Hussars. As a neutral from the Republic he could have gone home, but said: "A country which gives me my living is worth fighting for."

He came back to captain the team which gave Matt Busby his first trophies, the FA Cup in 1948 and the Championship in 1952, as well as playing for both the Republic of Ireland and Northern Ireland and captaining the Rest of Europe against Great Britain in a match to mark the end of hostilities.

As was to be expected, he went into management and was with Blackburn Rovers, Everton, Leyton Orient, Nottingham Forest and Blackburn again over a 16-year period before taking a job in the Borough Treasurer's office at Sale Town Hall.

PROFILE

BORN Dublin
DATE OF BIRTH 23 February 1919
JOINED UNITED November 1936
FEE £200
PREVIOUS CLUBS Home Farm, St James's Gate
UNITED LEAGUE APPS 306
GOALS 17

> "I can't recollect him ever getting annoyed, not even if someone had kicked him. He seemed to stroll through games. If he was playing today he would be called laid-back. Then we just thought he was unflappable."
>
> JOHN DOHERTY

STUART PEARSON

Stuart Pearson led Manchester United's great escape from the Second Division, shooting the Reds back into the big time at the first attempt.

Tommy Docherty realised he needed more gaols after presiding over relegation in season 1973–74 when the top scorer was Sammy McIlroy with a paltry total of six.

His response was to go back to one of his previous clubs, Hull City, and pay £200,000 for Pearson who had joined his local team as a youngster while also learning a trade as a telephone engineer. He had a good track record, topping the Hull scoring list for three seasons before his transfer.

He took the step up in his twinkling stride, scoring 17 goals in the promotion campaign to give his new club a speedy return to the First Division: for not only did he give United their first successful scorer for three years, but he lit the touch-paper for those around him, so that Lou Macari doubled his scoring rate to 11 and Gerry Daly also found himself among the goals.

The scoring continued in the First Division, rekindling memories of George Best and Denis Law, especially when the Doc restored faith in wingers and put Gordon Hill and Steve Coppell on the flanks. Pearson thrived as the leader of a swashbuckling attacking side, delighting fans with his flicks and deft turns.

In all he made 138 League appearances in four seasons and scored 55 goals. Along the way he won 15 England caps as well as appearing in two FA Cup finals.

Knee injuries put him out of the team and a new manager had other plans. Dave Sexton wanted to build his team around a strike-force of Jimmy Greenhoff and Joe Jordan, and the writing was on the wall when it came to a new contract.

Sexton said he knew nothing about promises made by Docherty and much better personal terms were on offer from West Ham, along with a £220,000 transfer bid. Stuart moved in August 1979 and was delighted to pick up a second FA Cup winner's medal with the Hammers the following year.

More knee injuries saw him released by the Hammers in 1982. He toured South Africa in Jimmy Hill's "rebel" team and played in the North American Soccer League before coaching at Stockport County, Northwich Victoria, West Bromwich and Bradford City.

Manchester remains his home, however, and he has resumed his association with Manchester United by working on the club's hospitality staff on match days as well as hosting the *Pancho Pearson* show on the United television channel.

"Pearson is a great player. He'll provide the spark that will set Old Trafford alight again, and he will play for England."

TOMMY DOCHERTY
ON SIGNING
STUART PEARSON

TONY DUNNE

I am pleased Tony Dunne has finished high in the voting because he was the original Quiet Man of Old Trafford and tended to go unnoticed.

Off the pitch he was hardly a headline-hunter. He just got on with his job. On the pitch it was exactly the same, he was so efficient he rarely stood out. He was hardly ever injured, even more rarely booked and almost never scored.

Yet in terms of his contribution to the cause, few have a better record. He made over 400 League appearances, played in 54 FA Cup ties and 40 European ties during one of the club's most successful eras.

He was probably taken for granted, which is perhaps why Tommy Docherty released him in 1973 and he was able to play nearly 200 games for Bolton. Although he runs a golf driving range in Altrincham just a few miles from Old Trafford, he rarely goes back there.

This lack of recognition certainly used to rankle at the time. I remember on a pre-season tour on the Continent finding him staring at a poster in our hotel for the forthcoming match.

In big letters it said: "Manchester United with Bobby Charlton, Denis Law, George Best etc."

He turned and said: "It's nice to be on the poster." I asked, "Where?", only for him to reply: "There I am: Etc Dunne. Nice name, isn't it?"

He had a point, because second billing was invariably his lot, yet few have a better record; and once you broke through the reserve he invariably had much to say for himself.

The Irish FA certainly thought so when he was part of a deputation which went over to Dublin to campaign for the appointment of a manager rather than relying on a committee to select and run the team. As he said at the time: "We want Irish football to be taken seriously."

He was also a trailblazer in the development of full-back play. For years the traditional backs had been strapping guys often with more strength than finesse. Even his predecessor Noel Cantwell was a well–built man, but with the arrival of Tony Dunne came a new breed of defender; small, wiry and exceedingly fast.

He credits Jimmy Armfield for the emergence of what he described as "little people" for the full-back position.

"Jimmy was not exactly small, but he was no giant and he was certainly fast," he explains. "He used his pace as part of his defence and also, in the modern style, to get forward down the flank to link up with the attack.

"He did this for England and was one of the first to be noticed because he took his style of play into the spotlight. I think he influenced a lot of managers."

Certainly I cannot watch Denis Irwin in the present United team without thinking that I saw this man nearly 40 years ago: fast, overlapping, neat, efficient, long-serving... and a quiet man.

PROFILE

BORN Dublin
DATE OF BIRTH 24 July 1941
JOINED UNITED April 1960
FEE £5,000
PREVIOUS CLUB Shelbourne
UNITED LEAGUE APPS 414
GOALS 2
INTERNATIONAL CAPS (Republic of Ireland) 33
GOALS 0

"He made over 400 league appearances, played in 54 FA Cup ties and 40 European ties during one of the club's most successful eras. Second billing was invariably his lot, yet few had a better record; and once you broke through the reserve, he invariably had much to say for himself."

FABIEN BARTHEZ

Many thought that Fabien Barthez faced Mission Impossible when he was signed, aged 28, for £7.8 million from French club Monaco in May 2000.

Stepping into the boots of the mighty Peter Schmeichel seemed such a mountain to climb, but the Frenchman quickly demonstrated that the Great Dane's reputation was not going to faze him.

It took less than a year for the readers of the Manchester United Magazine to vote him into the top half of the survey to decide the club's 100 Greatest Players. Fabien wasted no time making it abundantly clear that anything his predecessor could do he could do, if not better, then at least as well!

Of course, character as well as ability was what Sir Alex Ferguson was looking for when Schmeichel decided he had had enough of the demanding life at United. It proved a tricky task, because first came the trauma of Mark Bosnich and Massimo Taibi before Sir Alex found a goalkeeper with the panache to take the Old Trafford stage in his stride.

At times Barthez left the fans hardly able to believe what they were seeing, for he takes what seem to be enormous risks. He may decide to dribble round an onrushing centre-forward rather than simply kick the ball clear.

Supporters soon realised that he was no ordinary goalkeeper, even allowing for the perceived wisdom which says that anyone choosing to play in that position must be slightly mad.

He lives dangerously but has the ability to get away with it and everyone understood what the manager meant when he said on the player's arrival at the club: "Apart from his obvious goalkeeping skills, he has the personality to play on the biggest stage.

"It is an area in which Peter Schmeichel excelled, for he too had a great personality. Fabien is a World Cup winner and has not only the personality but the vast experience that is required at Manchester United."

United followers possibly became aware of the eccentric player when he was winning the World Cup with France in 1998 and was kissed on his bald pate for good luck by Laurent Blanc before the start of every match.

They could hardly miss the photographs in the papers featuring him with his former girlfriend, supermodel Linda Evangelista. As I say, he is different from most and he has lived up to his confident statement of intent made at the time of his transfer.

"I will need all my strength to replace Peter Schmeichel," he declared.

"He was a great 'keeper, a giant of a man; undoubtedly he was the best of his time. He played eight years with United and won everything, but I am confident I can fill the gap he left. I am as good a 'keeper now as I've ever been. I will wear the Manchester United shirt with pride and make the fans happy. I'm here to win. I've won championships with Monaco, the European Cup with Marseille and the World Cup with France and I want to carry on winning."

He probably will, too!

NOEL CANTWELL

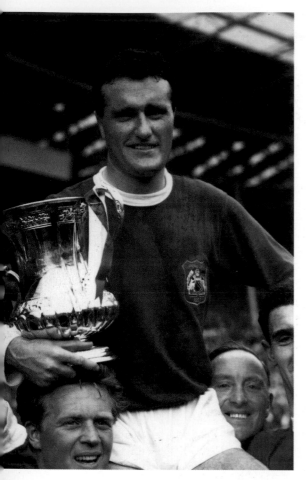

Noel Cantwell was the thinking man's footballer, principally because he was a thinking player himself.

Noel came from that hothouse of strategists who were trying to set the soccer world alight at West Ham during the late Fifties. Men like Malcolm Allison, John Bond, Malcolm Musgrove, Dave Sexton, Frank O'Farrell and Bobby Moore used to gather after training at a little café called Casetari's round the corner from the ground.

There they would move the salt and pepper pots round the table as they discussed tactics. It was a finishing school for future managers. Indeed, three of them went on to become either a manager or coach at Old Trafford, and Noel Cantwell was always one of the leading disciples among Upton Park's footballing freethinkers, so much so that when Matt Busby paid West Ham a then record fee for a full-back of £29,500, the transfer came as something of a culture shock.

The Cork-born Irishman, intelligent, articulate and full of ideas about the game, couldn't wait for the opportunity to learn from the most respected manager in football and get down to talking about the way forward with his illustrious new team-mates.

He had a long wait because, sadly for Noel, Manchester United were not that kind of club. Busby didn't believe in smothering his players with tactics. He relied instead on their intuition and concentrated on gathering round him players with the natural talent to express themselves, rather than trying to recall instructions from a dossier.

Noel, perhaps slightly disillusioned, nevertheless fitted in perfectly at left-back and was captain of the side through a testing time; for this was the crucial period after the Munich crash when, having steadied the ship by signing players like Ernie Taylor, Albert Quixall and Maurice Setters, Busby had to build further if he was to get back among the honours.

Cantwell arrived in November 1960 and more than played his part in leading United to their first trophy after the disaster. He was the defensive cornerstone and with the help of later arrivals, like David Herd, Denis Law and Pat Crerand, United rose superbly to the occasion as underdogs in the 1963 FA Cup final against Leicester City.

It was the launch-pad for the great era of the Sixties, and though Noel Cantwell faded before the later Championship successes, he was instrumental in bridging the barren years after the air crash. A natural choice as chairman of the Professional Footballers Association, many thought he would succeed Matt Busby, but instead he became manager of Coventry City as well as enjoying a spell as manager of the Republic of Ireland. He later managed in the USA and at Peterborough where he settled and ran a pub for some time. For the last two years he has been part of Dave Sexton's FA team scouting and writing international reports for England.

PROFILE

BORN Cork, Republic of Ireland
DATE OF BIRTH 28 February 1932
JOINED UNITED November 1960
FEE £29,500
PREVIOUS CLUBS Cork Athletic, West Ham
UNITED LEAGUE APPS 123
GOALS 6
INTERNATIONAL CAPS 36
GOALS 14

"Noel, perhaps slightly disillusioned, nevertheless fitted in perfectly at left-back to become the obvious man to captain the side through a testing time – the crucial period after the Munich crash. He more than played his part in leading United to their first trophy after the disaster."

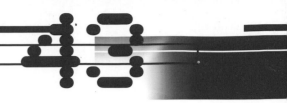

BRIAN KIDD

It's difficult to be sure whether Brian Kidd will be remembered more as a player or as a coach with Manchester United.

Certainly his career is closely woven into two great eras of the club's history.

As a player, he joined United as a youngster from St Pat's, the famous football school in Collyhurst which also launched Nobby Stiles, and Sir Matt Busby gave him his head after a tour of Australia. A strong, well-built striker, he scored United's third goal in the 1968 European Cup final against Benfica. There can surely be few better ways of celebrating your 19th birthday!

Still a young player, Kidd then seemed to become overwhelmed by the managerial strife following Sir Matt's retirement, and following relegation Tommy Docherty sold him to Arsenal for £110,000.

His career picked up again and he figured in three more big-money transfers to take in Manchester City, Everton and Bolton. He played for a number of teams in the States before management took him to Barrow, Swindon and Preston.

He seemed to be going nowhere significant, however, and returned to Old Trafford to work in community football. That led him into youth development with the club itself and a key role when Sir Alex Ferguson decided to revamp the scouting and coaching set-up.

United were lagging behind Manchester City in the youth stakes but Kidd worked hard and used his local knowledge to lay the foundations for the sudden rush of talent which would later supply half the United and England teams.

When Archie Knox suddenly upped sticks and went back to Scotland to join Glasgow Rangers as coach, Brian found himself asked to take over. He began to take the first-team coaching sessions and by the time of the European Cup Winners' Cup final against Barcelona in Rotterdam everything was functioning smoothly again.

Ferguson officially appointed him assistant manager and coach, and said: "It was a big shock when Archie decided to leave, but I reached the conclusion that Brian Kidd would grow into the job.

"He had done a fantastic job for me signing local schoolboys and I thought he could handle senior coaching. He was a big player himself, which helps wins the respect of senior players. His training routines have been excellent and he played a key part in our championship successes."

He certainly enjoyed the respect of one very senior star. "What a joy it is to train under him. There is more than quality in what he does, there is love," declared Eric Cantona.

In the year 2000, after flirting with the possibility of becoming Manchester City's manager, he left to manage Blackburn Rovers, only to quit after relegation.

He came back into football as youth coach at Leeds, later promoted by David O'Leary to coach the first team.

PROFILE

BORN Collyhurst, Manchester
DATE OF BIRTH 29 May 1949
JOINED UNITED August 1964
FEE None
PREVIOUS CLUB Junior
UNITED LEAGUE APPS 203
GOALS 52
INTERNATIONAL CAPS (England) 2
GOALS 1

"What a joy it is to train under him. There is more than quality in what he does, there is love."
ERIC CANTONA

"He was a big player himself which helps win the respect of senior players. His training routines have been excellent and he played a key part in our championship successes."
SIR ALEX FERGUSON

PAUL McGRATH

Paul McGrath was one of the most controversial and surprising characters to play for Manchester United.

He was a late starter in the professional game and he never ceased to surprise throughout his career. There was little indication as a schoolboy that he would go on to become one of the most talented centre-halves to wear the red shirt and become a key man for the Republic of Ireland.

As he put it himself: "I was 22 and still playing for St Pat's back home in Inchicore and I was as surprised as anyone when I got the invitation to go over to Old Trafford. I thought I had missed the boat. As a youngster I had always dreamed of being a professional footballer, but as time went on and no call, it seemed my chance had gone.

"I hadn't stood out as a youngster. I played for my school and I was once approached about a schoolboy trial, but nothing ever happened. I played for St Pat's for two years but we were all part-timers. I worked as a security guard, with football just a sideline."

Things certainly started to happen once he was at Old Trafford. He arrived easy-going but soon toughened up mentally and physically to make his debut six months after coming to Manchester.

He was on his way, a modest £30,000 buy dubbed "The Black Pearl of Inchicore" by his local paper when he went back to Ireland on a tour with his new club. As he modestly explained: "Not many lads from Inchicore get to play in the English First Division."

He proved to be one of Ron Atkinson's shrewdest buys as he went on to win an FA Cup winner's medal in a final against Everton and sustain an international career which brought him 83 caps.

Though twice voted Player of the Year by United fans, life never ran smoothly for the big Irishman. A succession of knee injuries laid him low and by the time Sir Alex Ferguson had taken over he was becoming just as well-known for drinking bouts and a car crash.

He asked United for a transfer because he said he was bored, and not long afterwards got his wish, as the new United manager set out to demonstrate that United were a football club rather than a drinking club.

He was sold to Aston Villa for £450,000 and then surprised everyone all over again by continuing to play despite the threat of his knees seizing up completely.

By simply playing rather than training he had seven years at Villa Park which, followed by a short spell with Derby, saw him still playing at the age of 38. Not bad for a player with dodgy knees!

Ferguson believes that it took the shock of his transfer to Villa to bring him to his senses. Certainly something did: he was voted PFA Player of the Year in 1993 and the following year was in the Villa side which beat United in the League Cup final.

PROFILE

BORN Ealing, London
DATE OF BIRTH 4 December 1959
JOINED UNITED April 1982
FEE £30,000
PREVIOUS CLUB St Patricks, Dublin
UNITED LEAGUE APPS 163
GOALS 12
INTERNATIONAL CAPS (Republic of Ireland) 83
GOALS 8

"I was 22 and still playing for St Pat's back home when I got the invitation to go over to Old Trafford. I thought I had missed the boat. As a youngster I had always dreamed of being a professional footballer, but it seemed my chance had gone."

PAUL McGRATH, UNABLE TO BELIEVE HIS LUCK

EDDIE COLMAN

They used to say that Eddie Colman had such a bewitching body swerve that he could send spectators in the stands the wrong way!

It may be a slight exaggeration, but he could certainly throw opponents off balance with his dummies and the dip of his shoulder. He could feint and swivel with the ball at his feet so adroitly that he became known as Snake Hips.

Salford born and bred, his father had been a well-known local player who had scored a hat-trick in the Salford Unemployed Cup final. Young Eddie was spotted by United as he worked his way up through the Salford Schoolboy team and the Lancashire side.

He became one of the exciting Busby Babes, first making his mark by playing in three FA Youth Cup-winning teams, and indeed becoming captain. He made his first-team debut aged 19 while he was still doing his National Service in the Royal Signals, and made such an impact that he quickly squeezed Jeff Whitefoot, himself a brilliant wing-half of great potential, out of the team.

It was no mean achievement. Whitefoot was such a good player that he went on to make nearly 300 appearances for Nottingham Forest and win an FA Cup final medal. There was no denying the talents of the young Colman, though, as he settled in at right-half to provide a contrasting balance with the muscular Duncan Edwards at left-half.

Chubby-faced, small and slightly-built, he was the opposite of Edwards, but size didn't come into it because he had such an instinctive talent. Indeed, the whole half-back line had a near-perfect balance. Both wing-halves were attack-minded but with Mark Jones, a traditional stopper centre-half between them, the team had an ideal mix.

Once Colman had come into the side the half-back line was virtually ever-present in the team which romped away with the Championship in 1955–56. It was a similar story the following year, with another great League title success.

The following year, with Jackie Blanchflower at centre-half, saw the team even more invincible, if that were possible, but of course in February 1958 tragedy struck at Munich. Colman, still only 21, was one of the eight killed, his cap and scarf found in the wreckage.

Always an impish player, he was a great favourite with the crowd and his tragically early death was deeply mourned in Salford where he was a popular figure who had not even had time to lose touch with his roots, and where he had become a much respected and much loved local hero.

PROFILE

BORN Salford
DATE OF BIRTH 1 November 1936
JOINED UNITED July 1952
FEE None
PREVIOUS CLUB Junior
UNITED LEAGUE APPS 85
GOALS 1
INTERNATIONAL CAPS (England) 0

> "Chubby-faced, small and slightly-built, he was the opposite of Edwards, but size didn't come into it because he had such an instinctive talent."

SAMMY McILROY

Sammy McIlroy was the last of the Busby Babes to come off the manager's famous youth production line, and he lived up to everything expected of a young man tutored by Sir Matt Busby.

> "I thought I would have found a few familiar faces in the lower divisions. I don't know why so many players pack up so early. The loss is theirs."
>
> SAMMY McILROY

He arrived at Old Trafford as a 15-year-old in 1969 and was there for the next 13 years, 11 of them as a first-team player. In all he served under five different United managers and gave them all unstinting service before going on to play for Stoke City, Manchester City and Bury.

He also had spells in Sweden and Austria as well as becoming player-manager at Preston and managing Macclesfield, before reaching the pinnacle of his career in the year 2000 when he was appointed manager of Northern Ireland.

As a player he carried on for as long as he could, as keen as ever, and baffled by the fact that most of his contemporaries no longer seemed to be around.

"I thought I would have found a few familiar faces in the lower divisions but they just weren't there," he said. "I don't know why so many players pack up so early. The loss is theirs.

"A promotion medal with Bury would have meant just as much to me as the FA Cup winners' medal I won with Manchester United. The pleasure was the same everywhere I played – provided I finished on the winning side, of course!

"The money wasn't as good at the end but playing was just as rewarding," said the man who won 89 caps for his country but felt there was always something new to learn in the game.

"At Bury we had to take our own kit home after training to be washed, so I learned how to work the washing machine," he said.

Sammy played through some traumatic times with United. He tasted life under Wilf McGuinness following Sir Matt's retirement and was given his League debut by Frank O'Farrell, the next manager.

He won't forget that experience in a hurry, after marking the occasion by scoring aged 17 in a derby at Maine Road.

His golden moment came after a night of despair because he had expected to play in the mini-derby for the reserves, a fixture traditionally played in those days on the Friday evening before the big match.

He was told that he wouldn't be playing and that instead he had to report to the first team the following morning, when he thought he would be on kit duty.

"I was very upset when Bill Foulkes, the reserve team coach, told me I wasn't in the side for the Friday night derby. I had been looking forward to it all week and I didn't think it was fair that I would have to go with the first team to help carry the kit baskets.

"So it came as a bit of a shock the next day when Denis Law failed a fitness test and manager Frank O'Farrell told me at 11 o'clock that I would be making my debut. Talk about excitement!"

HARRY GREGG

Harry Gregg was a great footballer but much more besides... like a hero!

It has never really been publicly recognised, but the Northern Ireland international emerged from the Munich air crash not only unscathed but also as a man who knew no fear.

For many years after the disaster there was a man who used to campaign for Harry to be awarded some decoration or medal for his heroism, but he never succeeded – mainly because the man who best knew what had happened simply refused to talk about it. Harry Gregg was a modest hero, and it wasn't until many years later that he acknowledged the part he had played in his dramatic rescue of a baby and her mother trapped inside the plane.

Harry escaped from the wreckage to be greeted by the pilot, Captain Thain, shouting for him to run because the plane was likely to explode, but just then he heard a baby crying. Ignoring the warning he went back in and crawled back out with the tiny baby girl. Then he went back in again to pull out the mother. He dragged Bobby Charlton and Dennis Viollet clear and tied his tie round Jackie Blanchflower's badly-bleeding arm.

To this day Harry says he doesn't know whether he was being brave or just too stupid to comprehend the danger. Either way, he was selfless and a good team-mate.

Given his reaction to a real emergency, it is no surprise to find him fearless in the game of football. Joining United from Doncaster just two months before the crash, he was the Northern Ireland goalkeeper in the team which reached the quarter-finals of the World Cup in 1958, and was named by FIFA as the best goalkeeper in the tournament.

Looking back now, he says: "I have

tremendous feeling for Manchester United. I might not go back there very often and twice I left when I didn't want to go. I didn't want to leave when I was transferred to Stoke City and the second time I had even less choice because I was sacked as a youth coach when Ron Atkinson took over.

"But nothing can spoil the happy memories. I still regard United as the Hollywood of football. I was part of the pre-Munich United, knowing and playing with the Busby Babes and Duncan Edwards. After Munich was difficult, but I like to think I did my best to help get the club through those rough times. Then I knew the era of Denis Law, Bobby Charlton, Paddy Crerand and George Best. I am proud of the fact that I persuaded Bertie Peacock to play George for Northern Ireland without him actually having seen him play."

After a career coaching and managing, Harry is back in Northern Ireland where he runs a hotel in Portstewart.

PROFILE

BORN Derry, Northern Ireland
DATE OF BIRTH 25 October 1932
JOINED UNITED December 1957
FEE £23,500
PREVIOUS CLUBS Coleraine, Doncaster Rovers
UNITED LEAGUE APPS 210
GOALS 0
INTERNATIONAL CAPS (Northern Ireland) 25
GOALS 0

"I might not go back very often, but nothing can spoil the happy memories. I still regard United as the Hollywood of football."

RELUCTANT HERO HARRY GREGG

DAVID HERD

David Herd would be a simply priceless player in the modern game because he could guarantee to score you 20 League goals a season, and do so consistently.

Sir Matt Busby brought him to Old Trafford from Arsenal for £35,000 in the summer of 1961 to replace Dennis Viollet as the process of rebuilding continued after Munich, and the new striker obliged by becoming top scorer with 14 League goals.

But once he had settled in and Denis Law had arrived a year later, David Herd reeled off seasonal totals of 19, 20, 20 and 24 before breaking his leg in March of the following season with his tally at 16 and every chance of making it his best year.

David Herd was overshadowed to a certain extent by the attractive talents of Law, his partner up-front, George Best and, of course, Bobby Charlton, but never underestimate his contribution. As Pat Crerand says, "David Herd was one of the most under-rated players ever to play for Manchester United."

As I say, clubs nowadays would die

for a striker who could give you five years averaging 20 League goals a season. He is, in fact, one of the select band of strikers who has averaged better than a goal every two games. In all competitions for United he scored 144 goals in 263 appearances. Two he will remember especially came in United's 3–1 FA Cup final victory over Leicester City before going on to become a key player in the Championship successes of 1965 and 1967.

His broken leg in March 1967 saw him fade from the picture before the European Cup success of '68, and it was perhaps typical that his injury happened in the act of scoring in the 5–2 League win against Leicester.

Always a tremendously hard kicker, he dispatched the ball with his usual venom, only to catch the boot of Graham Cross as his opponent came sliding in. You could see his foot hanging at an angle, and his United career was as good as over.

Goals always came naturally to David, who had the distinction as a 15-year-old of playing in the same Stockport County side as his 39-year-old father Alex, who in turn had played in the same Manchester City team as Matt Busby.

After five years at Edgeley Park he moved to Arsenal for £8,000, and just before returning north scored 30 goals to finish second to Jimmy Greaves as the First Division's top scorer.

After United he had two years at Stoke. Like many a United player of that era, he stayed in the area to establish a successful garage business in Davyhulme and continue his cricket career with local clubs like Cheadle Hulme, Timperley and Brooklands. He is also a keen committee man with the Association of Former Manchester United Players.

PROFILE

BORN Hamilton, Scotland
DATE OF BIRTH 15 April 1934
JOINED UNITED July 1961
FEE £35,000
PREVIOUS CLUBS Stockport County, Arsenal
UNITED LEAGUE APPS 263
GOALS 144
INTERNATIONAL CAPS (Scotland) 5
GOALS 4

"David Herd was overshadowed to a certain extent by the attractive talents of Law, his partner up-front, George Best and, of course, Bobby Charlton, but never underestimate his contribution. As Pat Crerand says, 'David Herd was one of the most under-rated players ever to play for Manchester United.'"

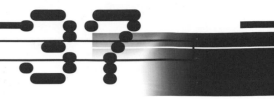

LOU MACARI

Lou Macari was always the joker in the pack: a non-smoker, an absolute non-drinker, but a guy who loved practical japes, especially if they meant discomfiture for the media.

It was the mischievous Scot who stole into the dressing-room at the Cliff training ground and cut the toes off the socks belonging to the Press team who had been lent the pitch for a day. Not content with that, though, the toe-ends later turned up stewing in the giant teapot used to provide a cuppa at the end of the game. Happily the newsmen were too exhausted to notice.

Lou Macari got on fine with the Press, but that did not prevent him on one away tour from clearing the clothes out of the bedroom of one reporter and hiding them for the next few days. In the meantime, forfeits had to be paid for the return of the belongings, with the result that at set times Her Majesty's gentlemen of the Press had to perform press-ups in the hotel lobby.

But once, the joking biter was bit! Tommy Docherty, another United man game for a laugh, spotted secretary Les Olive's briefcase by his chair at the airport as the club waited to fly home after a pre-season tour in Europe. With the official looking the other way, the Doc suggested Lou should hide the case in a toilet cubicle. Macari didn't need any encouragement and he quickly reported back that the mission had been accomplished. "Good," said the manager. "That'll give Les a surprise – his briefcase has all the cash takings in it from the tour."

A worried Macari then moved faster than he had done on the pitch as he legged it back to the gents' to retrieve something a little more valuable than the secretary's pyjamas and toothbrush!

All good fun, of course, and it certainly did not detract from Macari's commitment to either football or Manchester United. It was just that his restless spirit could not do with endless games of cards or TV during the long pauses between training and games.

Tommy Docherty had a rapid hire-and-fire policy when he arrived as manager of Manchester United, realising that drastic action was needed to rebuild an ageing team, and Lou Macari was one of the first players he recruited, paying Glasgow Celtic £200,000 to pull off a remarkable deal. It looked as if Liverpool had snapped him up after he attended one of their games, but he changed his mind. Lou Macari was always his own man, and though other players came and went, Lou stayed for 11 years.

It was a critical period for Manchester United, and though Macari won only one trophy – the 1977 FA Cup – he was one of the players who kept the club afloat, so despite relegation to the Second Division he was one of the main reasons they came roaring straight back up again.

He was a first-class player, of course. With Celtic he enjoyed two Scottish Championship successes and won two Scottish Cup medals. He also made 24 appearances for Scotland. Initially a striker, he switched later to more of a midfield role, and after the Doc he played for Dave Sexton until the arrival of Ron Atkinson and a move to Stoke as player-manager.

He made his name as a manager with Swindon, taking them from the Fourth Division to the Second on a shoestring. Since then he has managed West Ham, Birmingham City, Stoke City, Celtic and Huddersfield in a career which has brought him legal problems mainly, one suspects, because he is still very much his own man.

PROFILE

BORN Edinburgh
DATE OF BIRTH 4 June 1949
JOINED UNITED January 1973
FEE £200,000
PREVIOUS CLUB Glasgow Celtic
UNITED LEAGUE APPS 329
GOALS 78
INTERNATIONAL CAPS (Scotland) 24
GOALS 5

"Macari got on fine with the Press, but that did not prevent him clearing the clothes out of the bedroom of one reporter and hiding them."

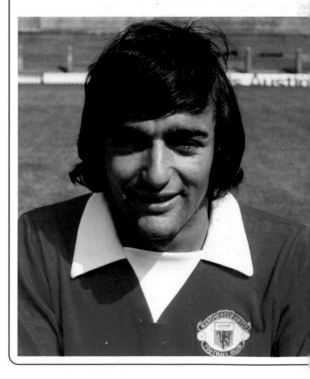

He has a keen sense of what is right and wrong, a quality that has also put him in demand as a match analyser for both television and radio.

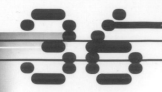

BRIAN McCLAIR

Brian McClair went from major star to bit-player in his 11 years with Manchester United. He played a support role for so long it seemed Sir Alex Ferguson was reluctant to see him leave the club.

Most fans came to regard him as the manager's favourite. And it is undoubtedly true that Ferguson did like having him around, and for a number of reasons. Brian McClair was a good professional: reliable, uncomplaining, versatile, never injured and an excellent influence in the dressing-room.

So it should be no surprise that, after playing for Motherwell and assisting Brian Kidd at Blackburn at the end of his playing days at Old Trafford, there is talk of him rejoining United this seaso as a junior coach.

That he finished his playing career at Old Trafford as something of an odd-job man should not disguise the fact that McClair made a highly significant contribution towards waking the sleeping giant and getting the Fergie revolution under way.

In his first season at United, following his £850,000 transfer from Glasgow Celtic in August 1987, he scored 24

League goals, the first United player to top 20 since the glory days of George Best in the Sixties.

To sit alongside the great marksmen of that era is no mean feat, because not all strikers have made the jump to the Old Trafford stage successfully.

He was Ferguson's first major signing and of course he came with a good reputation in front of goal after scoring 41 goals in 57 appearances in his last season at Parkhead.

Perhaps his secret was that he had the right attitude to the challenge, as he explained to me on his arrival: "I know people are looking for goals from me. I'm a fan myself and it is only natural. I don't resent it, and it doesn't bother me."

He duly went out and scored the goals that gave United the first three trophies under Ferguson, the FA Cup, European Cup Winners' Cup and League Cup. But the former university student who gave up his studies to go full-time with Motherwell remained just as laid-back, positive and enthusiastic through thinner years until he reached a season when he made just one appearance in the starting line-up.

How did the player nicknamed "Choccy" for the rhyme of his name with éclair then motivate himself?

"No problem. The motivation is the thought of what it would be like not to be with Manchester United. That's what gets me of a morning, and trying just as hard in training as I ever did. There are so many positive things about being at Old Trafford. You stand on the pitch and look round and, even if I am a substitute, I just think how marvellous it is to be involved in the European Champions League."

> "The motivation is the thought of what it would be like not to be with Manchester United. That's what gets me of a morning, and trying just as hard in training as I ever did."
>
> BRIAN McCLAIR EXPLAINS HIS ATTITUDE TO BEING A SUBSTITUTE

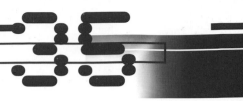

ALEX STEPNEY

United fans would forgive Alex Stepney anything. Even when their hero of the 1968 European Cup triumph crossed the great divide to become Peter Reid's goalkeeping coach at Manchester City, they still voted him an all-time Great, and they probably even felt sympathetic when he was sacked this summer along with Joe Royle.

A lex became a true Manchester man once he had accepted Sir Matt Busby's invitation to come to Old Trafford from Chelsea soon after the start of season 1966–67. Alex has never moved from his adopted North, living for a lot of the time in Rochdale.

Born in Mitcham in Surrey, he started in the amateur ranks of Tooting and Mitcham before he was snapped up by Millwall. He was still a long way from European glory, though, when Millwall were relegated to the Fourth Division in 1964. But their lean, lithe goalkeeper helped them bounce back at the first attempt and then into the Second Division.

His talent stood out and he was called up for three England Under-23 appearances. Alex also caught the attention of Tommy Docherty, the manager of Chelsea, who signed him for a then goalkeeping record fee of £50,000. The Doc had only signed him as cover for an unsettled Peter Bonetti. Once Bonetti had made up his mind to stay Alex became available and, after only four months, he was on his way to join United. The Doc sold him for £55,000, a further record for a keeper. Busby put him straight into the team in mid September to succeed Harry Gregg and David Gaskell, and watched his team race away with the 1966–67 Championship.

The team won the European Cup the following year, with Stepney a key man, especially when he pulled off a remarkable save against Eusebio in the final against Benfica. As Sir Matt said, "I thought as Eusebio raced towards him that all my dreams of winning the European Cup were going to be shattered. He shot with all his power but Alex held it."

In 12 seasons at Old Trafford Stepney made 433 League appearances and played in another 100 Cup games. He also achieved the rare distinction for a goalkeeper of scoring two League goals, called up in the relegation season to score two penalties.

PROFILE

BORN Mitcham, Surrey
DATE OF BIRTH 18 September 1942
JOINED UNITED September 1966
FEE £55,000
PREVIOUS CLUBS Tooting and Mitcham, Millwall, Chelsea
UNITED LEAGUE APPS 433
GOALS 2

ASKED FOR THE KEY FACTOR IN THEIR 1967 CHAMPIONSHIP SUCCESS, SIR MATT BUSBY SAID,

"Signing Alex Stepney. I only saw him play once for Millwall but it was enough. I kept the picture at the back of my mind... when I decided we needed a new goalkeeper I knew he was the man."

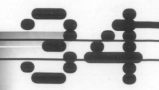

RONNY JOHNSEN

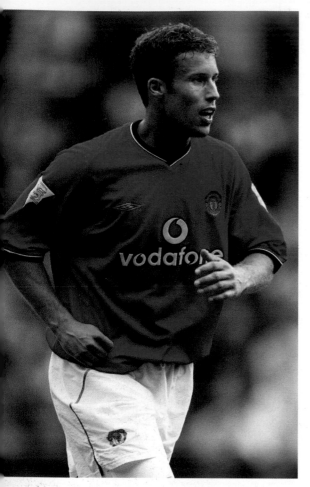

Injury has done its best to wreck the career of Ronny Johnsen, but nothing can diminish the valuable contribution he has made to United's success story under Sir Alex Ferguson.

The United manager could see problems ahead as the long-serving and solid defensive partnership of Steve Bruce and Gary Pallister broke up with the departure of Bruce. His answer was to launch a Viking raid of his own.

He looked to Norwegian football in the summer of 1996 and, in addition to picking up a bright young forward in Ole Gunnar Solskjaer, he tracked down Johnsen who at the time was playing in Turkey.

Johnsen found himself centre-stage after crushing defeats soon after his arrival, when United lost 5–0 at Newcastle and six days later crashed 6–3 at Southampton. The Norwegian international won a regular place to mark his first season with 37 competitive appearances and a Championship medal.

He continued to play a defensive role alongside players like Pallister, David May and Henning Berg, as well as linking up with Jaap Stam to share in the unique experience of the treble in season 1998–99.

He played in both of the cup finals and he was there when the Premiership was clinched against Spurs in the last League game.

Some foreign players take a while to settle, but Johnsen is something of a travelling man and maybe his year in Turkey enabled him to come to terms with English football quicker than most.

The player explained: "I had played for three senior clubs in Norway before the invitation came from Besiktas. They had a German trainer and I think he was looking outside Turkey for players and he had seen me playing for Norway.

"It was a challenge for me at the age of 26 and I thought, 'Why not try it?' It was quite an experience and good for me as a player.

"Turkish football is quite different but the Norwegian game is similar to the English style so I did not find it too difficult to adjust, except to say that a lot of the games in England are played at a great tempo with few rest periods."

Sadly for Johnsen, injury struck with a vengeance just when he seemed to have the football world at his feet. The season after the unique treble, he played in only two senior games, a victim of "jumper's knee".

He had, in fact, played through a pain barrier as the condition in his knee developed and he says: "To win the treble was fantastic and great to be involved, but the agony did spoil the enjoyment a bit for me."

Surgery on both knees and a slow recovery meant a year wiped out, and even the following season found Johnsen battling against various other injuries and making very few appearances.

PROFILE

BORN Sanderfjord, Norway
DATE OF BIRTH 10 June 1969
JOINED UNITED July 1996
FEE £1.6m
PREVIOUS CLUBS Lillestrom (Norway), Besiktas (Turkey)
UNITED LEAGUE APPS 89
GOALS 6
INTERNATIONAL CAPS (Norway) 43
GOALS 0

"Sadly, injury struck with a vengeance just when he seemed to have the football world at his feet. The season after the unique treble, he played in only two senior games, a victim of 'jumper's knee'."

BILL FOULKES

Bill Foulkes was the rock upon which Sir Matt Busby built the recovery of Manchester United after the Munich disaster.

In fact Big Bill, as this strapping centre-half became known to his team-mates, was a symbol of the post-Munich rebuilding because he had been in the crash himself.

He emerged somewhat traumatised but physically with hardly a scratch, and along with Harry Gregg carried on playing to keep the flag flying as Jimmy Murphy got a team together to play Sheffield Wednesday in the FA Cup just 13 days after the accident.

Other survivors joined in later in the season but Foulkes was there at the start to become a key player in the dramatic struggle to keep Manchester United going. He and Gregg were the foundations for a recovery which was so incredible that Sir Matt Busby was able to return and create another team. Bill Foulkes bridged the gap from the Busby Babes destroyed at Munich through the rebuilding years to complete the circle and enjoy the European triumph of 1968.

As he said: "I had come the whole way with the Boss trying to make Manchester United the champions of Europe. I thought the destruction of our team at Munich would have been the end of it, but he patiently put together another side.

"I'm proud to have been a part of it, and for those of us who lost our friends coming home from a European tie in 1958, our victory seemed the right tribute to their memory."

Perhaps it helped that Bill came from sturdy stock, his father a miner at St Helens as well as playing for the town team at Rugby League.

Bill also worked down the mine and was recruited playing for Whiston Boys'

Club at the age of 17, though only as a part-timer. Two years' National Service in the Army didn't help, but eventually he made his debut against Liverpool and went on to make 566 League appearances, a club record until overtaken by Sir Bobby Charlton.

He scored only nine goals in his United career, but one of them was against Real Madrid in Spain to win the semi-final on aggregate and put United through to the final against Benfica and ultimate glory in 1968. Bill was the unlikely scoring hero, but perhaps an appropriate one.

He followed his playing days by coaching the junior teams at Old Trafford for a period, as well as managing in the United States, Norway and Japan. The first chairman of the Association of Former Manchester United Players, he still lives in Sale representing Japanese football interests in this country and working for the Football for Life programme helping youngsters who fail to make the grade at professional clubs.

> "Bill Foulkes bridged the gap from the Busby Babes destroyed at Munich and through the rebuilding years to comlete the circle and enjoy the European triumph of 1968."

NICKY BUTT

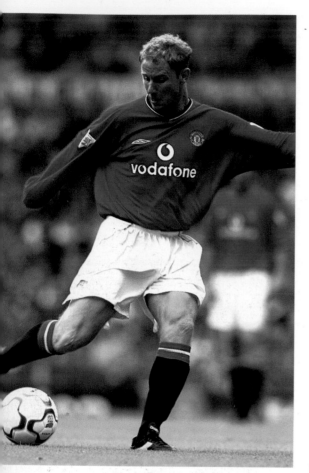

It was a big decision when Sir Alex Ferguson decided to let Paul Ince leave for Italy, but he did so in the knowledge that he had Nicky Butt waiting in the wings.

In fact Butt was one of the first to break through to senior level from the talented class of '92 to form a midfield partnership with Roy Keane.

Later, he found the going harder, as Paul Scholes arrived to challenge for a midfield position. For a long time the more attack-minded Scholes with his scoring flair was favoured for home fixtures, Butt coming into the reckoning away from home, when the emphasis might be more on defensive strength.

Occasionally they would form the midfield pair together, especially in the season Keane missed through injury, but afterwards it often seemed to be head-to-head between Butt and Scholes for a place in the team.

Sir Alex Ferguson describes Butt as the loyal soldier and says: "I don't always pick Nicky to start in a match and, at times, the situation makes me feel guilty. At any other club he would be a first-choice player all the time. He never lets you down with his consistency and determination."

How does he react to being described as "a loyal soldier"? Perhaps he feels the manager takes advantage of his uncomplaining approach?

Says Butt: "We all accept the squad system and generally speaking the club is so successful in the different competitions that there are plenty of appearances for everyone. Very few are going to get through the whole season playing in every match.

"I'm happy at Old Trafford, and if I am regarded as a patient, loyal player, that's fine by me. I don't think I could handle all the star treatment and hassle someone like David Beckham gets."

Nicky, who grew up locally in Gorton, joined United in 1991 after the manager had shaken up the scouting system to bring in more local boys. He made his first-team debut at 17 and says: "I haven't had much to complain about. When I first joined the manager made it clear that if you were good enough you would get your chance, and quite a few of us have."

The stop–go aspect of his club career has possibly hindered his international selection and after a bright start for England he was disappointed to miss out on selection for France 98.

"I was upset, but it was never a certainty that I would be in the team and so I was not disheartened," he explained. "As soon as I was back with my family and friends I put it to the back of my mind and two days after getting home to Manchester I went off on holiday to Barbados."

It was a typically laid-back response from a player who has never faltered in his commitment to United, and it was a fitting reward that Sven-Göran Eriksson immediately made him part of his England squad when he took over as manager.

PROFILE

BORN Manchester
DATE OF BIRTH 21 January 1975
JOINED UNITED July 1991
FEE None
PREVIOUS CLUB Junior
UNITED LEAGUE APPS 206
GOALS 19
INTERNATIONAL CAPS 14
GOALS 0

NOBBY STILES

Nobby Stiles danced his way into the hearts of football fans everywhere when he celebrated England's World Cup victory over Germany at Wembley in 1966.

With his socks round his ankles and an ear–splitting grin revealing the absence of his front teeth, the Manchester United man jigged joyfully round the pitch into the affections of people who knew they had just seen a footballer who had played his heart out for his country.

While never the most elegant of performers, it was the only way he knew how to play and, coupled with his outstanding ability to read the game, he was a key member of United's defence through the successful Sixties.

Sir Matt Busby valued him enormously, and so did Sir Alf Ramsey who consistently selected him to knit together the more sophisticated thoroughbreds of his World Cup-winning team.

Ramsey played him just in front of his central defenders, Bobby Moore and Jack Charlton. Busby had him mostly alongside Bill Foulkes. In both roles he was a ball-winner and provider of the simple pass, always showing an uncanny knack for spotting a threat. Sir Bobby Charlton once told me his pal reminded him of a sheepdog, constantly rounding up those who strayed out of line and barking at them until they were back in the pen!

Of course he snapped at a few heels to do it and undoubtedly had a fierce tackle, though Bobby Charlton always used to insist that some of his mistimed efforts were down to poor eyesight. "He didn't tackle people so much as just bump into them," he said. Matters improved after Nobby discovered contact lenses.

Certainly opponents did not take liberties with him and fans abroad hated him. He was hit on the head by a bottle in Madrid, hissed and spat at in Italy and described as an assassin in South America.

In fact, when United arrived at Buenos Aires airport to play Estudiantes for the World Club Championship, the welcoming commentator boomed over the public address system: "Bobby Charlton, El Supremo, George Best, El Beatle," and then with his voice rising an octave: "Nobby Stiles, El Bandido!"

He played first-team football at Old Trafford for 11 seasons after joining as a young apprentice and making his debut at the age of 18. He played nearly 400 games before suffering the effects of two cartilage operations, which brought his United career to an end at the age of 27.

He was far from finished, though, and went to Middlesbrough for £20,000.

Unlike the hostile reception accorded to most players returning to their old clubs, there were welcoming banners for him when he arrived back with Middlesbrough, and he was given the warmest of welcomes, still as popular as ever.

He moved on to Preston where he was successively player, coach and manager.

He also coached in Canada and at West Bromwich before Sir Alex Ferguson brought him back to Old Trafford as a junior youth coach.

His popularity and success – very few players have won both World Cup and European Cup winners' medals – eventually drew him into a full–time career as an after-dinner speaker and he found he had to give up his United post.

"Never the most elegant of performers, it was the only way he knew how to play, and he was a key member of United's defence throughout the successful Sixties."

PROFILE

BORN Manchester
DATE OF BIRTH 18 May 1942
JOINED UNITED September 1957
FEE None
PREVIOUS CLUB Juniors
UNITED LEAGUE APPS 311
GOALS 17
INTERNATIONAL CAPS (England) 28
GOALS 1

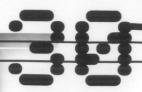

PAT CRERAND

It was often said that when Pat Crerand played well, Manchester United played well.

PROFILE

BORN Glasgow

DATE OF BIRTH 19 March 1939

JOINED UNITED February 1963

FEE £53,000

PREVIOUS CLUB Glasgow Celtic

UNITED LEAGUE APPS 304

GOALS 10

INTERNATIONAL CAPS
(Scotland) 16

GOALS 0

And almost invariably this was the case because the former Glasgow Celtic midfielder was a play-maker before the term was even invented. In fact it was the Scot's ability to create that prompted Sir Matt Busby to bring him down from Celtic Park for a fee of £53,000 in February, 1963.

The attack featuring David Herd and

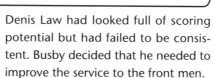

"The former Glasgow Celtic midfielder was a play-maker before the term was even invented."

Denis Law had looked full of scoring potential but had failed to be consistent. Busby decided that he needed to improve the service to the front men.

It was one of his shrewdest decisions. Not only did he have the right balance in the half-back line with Maurice Setters on one flank and Crerand, a player of vision, on the other, he now had a man to pass the right kind of ammunition for Law and Herd to fire. It was the proverbial final piece of the jigsaw. Crerand arrived too late to do much about the League position, but in the FA Cup that season there developed a pattern and a glimpse of better days ahead.

United got through every round without needing a replay and after beating Southampton 1–0 at Villa Park in the semi-final they faced Leicester City in the final.

Leicester, doing well in the League that season, were clear favourites and were expected to swamp a team heading for a finishing place of 19th in the League table.

It was the match in which Crerand come into his own. Wembley suited him and he destroyed the Leicester midfield in a link-up with Law which was a firm indication of things to come.

A perfect pass from Crerand enabled Law to score the first goal, with Herd scoring twice for a 3–1 victory.

Manchester United and Pat Crerand were on their way, as they visibly showed the following season by finishing runners-up in the First Division and reaching the FA Cup semi-finals.

The next three seasons brought them two Championships and the European Cup with Crerand at the heart of their super side of the Sixties. It was sometimes said he was slow, and a favourite jibe from the after-dinner speakers these days is that he had two speeds, slow and stop! But the remark doesn't do justice to his creative skills.

Crerand also had his fiery moments. He wasn't a hatchet man, but if fouled, his retribution tended to be dramatic and swift. He once escaped a ban for hitting an opponent on the grounds that he had only struck him once and that that hardly constituted fighting; what was not said was that nothing more was ever needed, as the foreign goalkeeper who never made it to the top of the tunnel after a European match could testify!

After a brief spell as assistant manager to Tommy Docherty at Old Trafford and a few other coaching posts, Pat remains a fervent United fan living not far from the ground, whose passion for the team always spills out in his work as a forthright radio pundit.

GARY NEVILLE

Gary Neville stood out as a future captain of Manchester United when he was directing operations in the team that won the FA Youth Cup in 1992.

This was the side which went on to form half the first team for United and England, with Gary always standing out as not only a very good footballer, but as a highly intelligent organiser.

It's perhaps not insignificant that his choice of newspaper for his fortnightly column is *The Times*, and as Sir Alex Ferguson says: "Gary accepts responsibility both on and off the field, which extends to organising a lot of dressing room commitments and representing his team-mates in talks with the club.

"As a footballer, it's been his determination and concentration which have got him to the highest levels for both club and country, and at either full back or in central defence."

The United manager has repeatedly switched Neville from one position to the other whenever he has had need. Centre half, where he played in the youth team, is his preferred position, but he has made most of his senior appearances at right back, where he has been a model of consistency.

Eric Harrison, his youth team coach, says: "He came to us as a midfield player but I could see he had a defensive brain and we moved him into the centre of defence where he was outstanding. However, there was a concern about his lack of height and in the end we switched him to full back to give him a better opportunity of getting into the first team. Changing his position was not a problem for him because if he knew there was something to be worked on, say a one-to-one situation with the winger, then he would work and work until he got it right."

Gary, who joined United from school in Bury, comes from a very sports orientated family with his father, Neville Neville, commercial director of Bury Football Club, where his mother is the secretary.

His younger brother, Philip, followed him into the first team to raise the possibility of them becoming England's regular full-back pair.

Jimmy Armfield, an FA adviser who in his day won 43 caps for England at right back, believes that the Nevilles could become the first international family partnership since Bobby and Jack Charlton starred for England in the Sixties.

"They have still got a bit to do to match the Charltons but it is a possibility. They are both impressive players and apart from their natural ability they have the temperament needed for football at the highest level," he says.

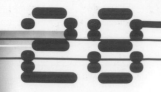

DENNIS VIOLLET

Dennis Viollet's narrow escape from death in the Munich air crash did nothing to blunt either a sharp sense of humour or a jaunty approach to life. Indeed those players who knew him before and after the crash say that survival seemed to make him even more determined to squeeze the last drop out of life.

As a fellow "Busby Babe," John Doherty, who grew up with him at Old Trafford, put it: "The effect of Munich on his life was that he mustn't waste a minute of what was left."

One can never be certain if Munich took anything away from Dennis Viollet as a player, though he had certainly made a dashing start before the air disaster as partner to Tommy Taylor in the swashbuckling forward line of the mid-fifties which won successive Championships and was making a big impact in Europe.

His silky, sharp and stealthy approach made him a perfect foil for Taylor, but he died at Munich and perhaps at the very top level something also went from Viollet's game.

Nevertheless, two seasons after Munich in an attack featuring Bobby Charlton, Alex Dawson and Albert Quixall, he scored 32 League goals from just 36 appearances, a club record which stood the test of time and at the time of writing has not been bettered.

It makes you wonder what he might have gone on to achieve, with a maturing Taylor by his side, for United and perhaps for England, too. As it was, he won only two caps. Perhaps the selectors were put off by his seemingly slight physique, but there was in fact steel in a wiry frame and he had an electric burst of speed to go with an astute mind, good timing and an instinctive vision.

Viollet grew up in Moss Side in the shadow of Manchester City. Indeed, it was no secret that as a boy he had been a City supporter, but it did not prevent him giving Matt Busby excellent service as well as a few headaches.

His scoring record for United – 178 goals from 291 games in all competitions – still speaks for itself. His former playing colleagues have nothing but admiration for his prowess. As John Doherty, his old team-mate, put it: "He would always be in my all-time best United eleven. The lack of caps was an insult."

There was still a lot of football left in him when he left United for Stoke. He sampled American football before returning to play for Linfield in Northern Ireland and for Ken Barnes at Witton Albion. He coached at Preston and Crewe before returning to America where he settled in a coaching capacity with Washington Diplomats and Jacksonville University.

He died in the States in 1999, after a brave fight against a brain tumour.

PROFILE

BORN Manchester
DATE OF BIRTH 20 September 1933
JOINED UNITED October 1947
FEE None
PREVIOUS CLUBS Junior
UNITED LEAGUE APPS 239
GOALS 159
INTERNATIONAL CAPS (England) 2
GOALS 1

"He was brilliant at timing his runs which together with great finishing made him one of the best inside lefts in the game. He was so full of guile and craft and certainly a crafty blighter to play against."

KEN BARNES, FORMER MANCHESTER CITY CAPTAIN

ROGER BYRNE

Roger Byrne knew his own mind, which is probably why he became not only an outstanding defender but a great captain.

He was a natural leader much respected by the Busby Babes as they began to pile into the team with their youthful enthusiasm. He was that little bit older because he had played in the 1952 League championship season. In fact only he and Johnny Berry bridged the gap from the old guard to the team that started to take over soon afterwards.

But his development as the leader of the Busby Babes did not happen overnight. As Sir Matt Busby once explained: "He was a strong-willed young man, and, as many young men are, he was a bit headstrong to begin with."

Indeed, after Byrne was sent off in a match on tour in America, Busby made him apologise to his predecessor as captain, Johnny Carey, for defying the skipper's instructions to stay calm.

Under threat of being sent home, Byrne duly apologised and Busby reckoned it was part of his growing up to become another of the club's outstanding captains.

Busby certainly had the greatest respect for him after converting him from left winger to full back, saying: "Simple proof of Byrne's outstanding skill is that I never saw either the great Stan Matthews or the great Tom Finney do anything against him. Greater tribute can no full back have than this. There was never a faster full back."

But Byrne was a relatively late arrival at Old Trafford. He played his junior football for a local team, Ryder Brow Youth Club, in Gorton, where his partner was Brian Statham, a player who eventually chose cricket ahead of football to become a brilliant pace bowler for Lancashire and England.

Roger Byrne also went close to being lured into another sport because when he did his two years National Service in the RAF he was overlooked for the Station soccer team and played rugby instead.

Happily he reverted to football after his service and at the age of 20 joined United in March, 1949, where he quickly made his way through the junior teams and reserves. He made his debut in season 1951–52 at full back and performed solidly, but it was towards the end of the season when he attracted major attention. Busby asked him to play in his original position at outside left to accommodate the return of John Aston to left back after injury, and Byrne became the hero of the hour. He scored seven goals in the last six games to clinch the League and give Busby his first Championship success.

After asking for a transfer the following season because he didn't like playing on the wing, he was returned to left back and it was clear he had found his true position, though his ability to raid forward from defence always remained one of his special qualities.

He was made captain in 1954 and two months later made his England debut. Byrne went on to play in 33 consecutive internationals before the Munich crash, which hurled him out of the broken aircraft. Team-mate Harry Gregg found him lying in the snow.

"He was dead but there wasn't a mark on him. He was always a handsome fellow, handsome in life and handsome in death," Gregg said.

Eight months after losing his life in the carnage, Byrne's wife, Joy, gave birth to their son – christened Roger in loving memory.

PROFILE

BORN Gorton, Manchester
DATE OF BIRTH 8 February 1929
JOINED UNITED March 1949
FEE None
PREVIOUS CLUB Gorton Brow Youth Club
UNITED LEAGUE APPS 245
GOALS 17
INTERNATIONAL CAPS (England) 33
GOALS 0

"There was never a faster full back."
SIR MATT BUSBY

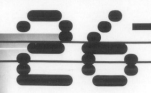

PAUL INCE

There was nothing ever straightforward about Paul Ince in his time with Manchester United. The trauma of his transfer from West Ham to Old Trafford in September, 1989, was complicated, and the manner of his departure four years later was similarly involved and controversial.

There were a few ups and downs in between, too!

His move North was certainly unusual when it was announced at the Press conference held to meet the new player that there was a medical hitch. The doctors had discovered a possible pelvic injury which meant the deal was on hold.

Insurance was the main problem, and as Sir Alex Ferguson said at the time: "The transfer came to a full stop. The boy took it badly. We all took it badly and it left us all in limbo."

One of the problems was that there was really no way back to Upton Park for Paul because by that time he had posed in London for a newspaper

PROFILE

BORN Ilford, London
DATE OF BIRTH 21 October 1967
JOINED UNITED September 1989
FEE £1.5m
PREVIOUS CLUB West Ham
UNITED LEAGUE APPS 206
GOALS 24
INTERNATIONAL CAPS (England) 42
GOALS 2

"He developed into a top-class player notable for his work-rate, his tackling and the vision of his defensive covering."

picture wearing a Manchester United shirt in anticipation of his move.

Eventually, United agreed to pay £500,000 down and the other £1m in instalments based on appearances. So he duly became a United man, though he needed time to come to grips with life at Old Trafford.

However, he developed into a top-class player notable for his work-rate, his tackling and the vision of his defensive covering. He became an integral part of midfield, eventually taking over from Bryan Robson to partner Roy Keane.

Ince was very much part of United's trophy charge, especially in the side which ended 26 years without the Championship in season 1992-93.

I remember one season he dominated the form ratings I used to award in the *Manchester Evening News* with a better average than even Eric Cantona, Mark Hughes and Steve Bruce. Indeed he was man of the match on 10 occasions in 48 appearances.

His international career also took off and in 1993 he was made captain of England against the United States. No wonder he began to let it be known that he liked to be referred to as "The Guv'nor" and acquired a car number plate with "Guv" on it.

His choice of epithet perhaps summed up the breakdown of his relationship with the manager, who accepted an £8m offer from Inter Milan just before the start of the 1995–96 season.

Sir Alex also suspected that the player had privately set his mind on playing abroad and felt it was the right time to be parting. No room for two Guv'nors at Old Trafford perhaps!

It was far from the end of his career, though, with transfers to Liverpool and Middlesbrough after two years in Italy.

ANDREI KANCHELSKIS

Andrei Kanchelskis had a stormy career at Old Trafford, unsettled when he was not in the team, and on a collision course at times with the manager.

There is no doubting, though, that at his peak he was an inspiring sight flying down the right wing, and the fans forgave him the fall-outs. Indeed, they were surprised, and many of them upset, when Sir Alex Ferguson sold him to Everton in 1995 after a season in which he had become the team's top scorer with 15 goals.

But to a great extent Kanchelskis was always a little boy lost after joining United from Shakhytor Donetsk in the Ukraine for £750,000 in May 1991.

When he was put on the plane for England he didn't even know whether he was being asked to join United or Manchester City. He spoke no English, and though United immediately appointed a Russian-speaking former university lecturer to help him, he was 21 and homesick. Even when he was joined by his girlfriend, Inna, later to become his wife, they had the misfortune to lose their new-born baby.

After two years his frustration at not playing regularly in the first team came to a head. He refused to play in the reserves, which did not exactly endear him to the United manager!

"All I was getting was a little run-out as a substitute towards the end of a match when it was too late to show what I could do," he said. "I was frustrated, upset and felt insulted, especially when the manager told me to play for the reserves... I played for the reserves twice but I was worried I might sink to that level if I did it too often... My lowest point came when I was out of the team and we lost our baby. We seemed to be a long way from home with everything going wrong."

Kanchelskis made his peace, though, and was in the team that won the Rumblelows Cup in 1992, then helped land the League and FA Cup double the following season.

No doubt he felt more settled in England with the arrival of his baby son, Andrei Andreivitch, but a hernia injury, along perhaps with his agent trying to get him to a new club, meant his United career ended in more acrimony.

No doubt finishing second in the League to Blackburn didn't help the manager's mood and suddenly Kanchelskis departed, along with Paul Ince and Mark Hughes, in a wave of controversy.

After Everton came a move to Fiorentina in Italy, a return to Britain to play for Glasgow Rangers, and then the wheel turned full circle to bring him to play for City at Maine Road.

"At his peak he was an inspiring sight flying down the right wing at great pace."

DWIGHT YORKE

Dwight Yorke is as well known at Old Trafford for his sunshine smile as he is for his remarkable talent in front of goal, and it is difficult to know which has lit up Old Trafford more since his £12m signing from Aston Villa in August 1998.

Yorke was the manager's answer to a season which had promised much but had delivered nothing in the way of trophies. Runners-up to Arsenal in the Premiership, a disappointing European exit against Monaco and a shock knock-out in the FA Cup at Barnsley was not what Sir Alex Ferguson had planned.

The result was a move for Yorke, the striker from Tobago who had been brought into English football by Graham Taylor after being spotted when Villa played there.

Yorke's response was better than even Ferguson could have hoped for as his team swept to their incredible treble with Yorke a star in all three competitions. The new signing was not only an instant individual success: he seemed to spark a renewed lease of life in Andy Cole and together they formed a wondrous partnership that looked as if they were scoring goals for fun.

Together they scored 53 goals in the treble season, with Yorke contributing 29 of them, and, not surprisingly, he won the Player of the Year accolade awarded by Carling, the Premier League sponsors.

"Andy and I have a good understanding. We hit it off right from the start both on and off the field," he said.

When he first arrived it seemed Cole would be more of a rival than a friend, and Yorke thought so, too: "I thought to myself that if there was one person I could have problems with, it was Andy Cole. All the talk was of me coming to Old Trafford while Andy moved on to make way for me. Yet the one person who took me under his wing and welcomed me to the club more than anyone else was Andy."

And what about his other trademark, the upturned collar?

"I started to do that when I was at Aston Villa... It was around the time Eric Cantona arrived wearing his collar up and I thought to myself, I like that. It's cool, I'll have some of that for me!" he laughed with another flash of his trademark smile, though he wasn't smiling quite as much during season 2000-01, when injuries and repeated international calls broke his rhythm and he found himself dropping down the pecking order of strikers.

PROFILE

BORN Canaan, Tobago
DATE OF BIRTH 3 November 1971
JOINED UNITED August 1998
FEE £12 million
PREVIOUS CLUBS Bertil School Tobago, Aston Villa
UNITED LEAGUE APPS 64
GOALS 38
INTERNATIONAL CAPS (Trinidad and Tobago) 39 (est.)
GOALS 20 (est)

"Yorke seemed to spark a renewed lease of life in Andy Cole and together they formed a wondrous partnership."

TEDDY SHERINGHAM

Football supporters don't miss a trick. They know a chant or a jibe that hurts and they are never slow to stick the knife in when they catch up with a player who has left them to join another club.

London fans, especially those from Tottenham, remembered all too clearly that when Sheringham left White Hart Lane to join Manchester United in the summer of 1997 he announced that he was moving North in a bid to win major medals.

But at first the honours proved elusive and, as Sheringham ruefully conceded at the time, "I know all the songs aimed at me about not winning anything and yes of course it needles, but I regard it as part of the challenge which I have got to rise to…. I am still confident in my ability, though. The job is not too big for me and my aim now is to turn things round," he said.

And turn them round he did, though not without a few more ups and downs, such as the signing of Dwight Yorke to add even more competition up front. Indeed, Yorke and Andy Cole formed a red-hot partnership which left Sheringham and Ole Gunnar Solskjaer with supporting roles rather than star billing.

Sheringham still hung in there, though, and certainly had the last laugh when he went on as a late substitute to equalise against Bayern Munich in the European Champions League final in May 1999, and set the scene for a sensational victory.

He marked the new millennium season by signing another contract and promptly hit red-hot form to emerge with a regular place and become the leading scorer, as well as returning to the international fold with England.

So has the well-travelled Londoner who arrived at Old Trafford via Millwall, Nottingham Forest and Spurs, any regrets about moving North?

"Not one," he replied. "I didn't win all that much with my other clubs and I certainly couldn't possibly have turned down the opportunity to join a great club like United. I like it here, too. I have been surprised. I honestly didn't expect to settle in so well."

His patience was certainly well rewarded in season 2000-01 when he not only emerged as the team's top scorer with over 20 goals, but was voted Player of the Year by both the football writers and his fellow professionals.

PROFILE

BORN Highams Park, London
DATE OF BIRTH 2 April 1966
JOINED UNITED June 1997
FEE £3.5m
PREVIOUS CLUBS Millwall, Aldershot (loan), Djurgaarden (loan), Nottingham Forest, Spurs
UNITED LEAGUE APPS 75
GOALS 16
INTERNATIONAL CAPS (England) 39
GOALS 9

"Playing for Manchester United is something special. Everyone tells you it's a big club, but … you don't really know what it is going to be like."

OLE GUNNAR SOLSKJAER

The Norwegian striker is not only a top-class striker but is loyal, uncomplaining and happy, the perfect player for a club like Manchester United.

Sir Alex Ferguson knows he must have a large pool of players if he is to maintain a challenge on all fronts. He rotates his players, but there can still be a problem with those he leaves out, and when everyone is fit, he can't pick them all.

Solskjaer would start every match at possibly any other club, but at Old Trafford he so often has to play second fiddle to contemporaries like Teddy Sheringham, Andy Cole and Dwight Yorke.

But he never protests and nor does he want to leave. Spurs pressed hard for him for a season leading up to the summer of 2000 and the United manager gave him the option to leave without any hard feelings because he had been so patient, but he turned his back on the chance.

He signed a seven-year contract in 1997, a year after joining United from Molde for £1.5m, and is consequently way down the pay league, but it still makes no difference.

"Money is not important. I can only live under one roof and within four walls. If money was all important I would not have signed for United in the first place," he explains.

"My love for United is greater than my need for more money. My dream is to finish my career with Manchester United. I don't want to play for any other clubs. I have had other offers, far better offers, but I fear any other club would be a tragic comedown for me. I hope when the time comes I'll get another contract and the chance to end my career at Old Trafford."

Of course Ole Gunnar has had moments to compensate for failing to start as regularly as some of the other players, not least in the 1999 final of the European Champions League against Bayern Munich in Barcelona.

He went on for the closing stages, then scored the winning goal in injury time, to complete a unique treble of trophies.

It must have been a sweet moment, though not really a surprise because in just over four years after signing in July 1996, he scored 70 goals from 184 appearances, 75 of which were as a substitute, sometimes on the field for just a few minutes.

As Ferguson says: "When he is through one-on-one I always feel confident. He is one of the best finishers of all time. His strike rate is second to none."

Ole Gunnar Solskjaer is a manager's dream, especially at a big club where the manager has built strength in depth and has to leave quality players on the substitutes' bench.

"He is one of the best finishers of all time. His strike rate is second to none."
SIR ALEX FERGUSON

PROFILE

BORN Kristiansund, Norway
DATE OF BIRTH 26 February 1973
JOINED UNITED July 1996
FEE £1.5m
PREVIOUS CLUBS Clausenengen FK, Molde
UNITED LEAGUE APPS 184
GOALS 70
INTERNATIONAL CAPS (Norway) 16
GOALS 8

GARY PALLISTER

All successful teams are strong in central defence and every manager's dream is to develop a partnership at the back which is not only reliable but durable, so that stability and understanding are created consistently at the heart of the team.

So when Sir Alex Ferguson launched a wave of rebuilding after finishing 13th in the League in 1988–89, he went to Middlesbrough to sign Gary Pallister as a partner for Steve Bruce, who had been at the club for only a season.

Negotiations went on until the small hours of the next day and left the United manager describing Colin Henderson, the Middlesbrough chairman, as the hardest man in Britain when it came to bargaining.

Ferguson suggested beforehand that they should offer £1.3m but be prepared to go to around £1.8m, only to be greeted at the start of the meeting by Gibson saying Boro wanted £2.3m or United could forget it.

Ferguson said the battle then started and they were in and out of the room like a fiddler's elbow before, six hours later, agreeing the fee originally demanded by Middlesbrough.

That left only one thing to settle: who would wake up United chairman Martin Edwards on holiday in Spain with the news that they had just agreed to fork out a club record fee considerably larger than planned?

In the event Gary Pallister proved a bargain buy, especially compared with Glenn Hysen, the Swedish defender who was nearly 30 and the man they had originally wanted, only to lose him to Liverpool. Hysen flopped and Liverpool lost their money, while Pallister went on to become the keystone, with Steve Bruce, of an outstanding defence which was the foundation for the most successful era in the club's history.

And then United sold Pallister, who had also become an experienced England international, back to Middlesbrough for £3.5m. Boro are not the only club who know how to strike a hard bargain!

Ferguson likened the player in his early days at Old Trafford to a new-born foal with no real physique apart from his height. Indeed, he had a shaky start and marked his debut against Norwich by conceding a penalty.

But he soon got the hang of Old Trafford's big stage, winning a medal every season to collect a rich haul of trophies. He returned to Middlesbrough in July, 1998, missing out on the treble, but he had done his job well and had proved very durable. For four successive seasons he made 50 or more appearances and in the double season of 1993–94 he topped 60. He had certainly answered a manager's dream.

"Pallister became the keystone with Bruce of an outstanding defence which was the foundation for the most successful era in the club's history."

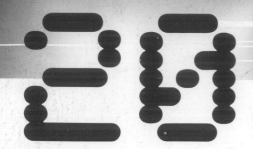

STEVE COPPELL

Steve Coppell was combining a degree in economic history at Liverpool University with football for lowly Tranmere Rovers when Bill Shankly turned his world upside down.

In his first year at University, Steve was playing in Tranmere's senior side as an amateur when he caught the eye of the former Liverpool manager who liked the way he had emerged as the Third Division club's top scorer with 12 goals in his first season.

Shankly recommended him to United with the words: "I have had quite a bit to do with Tranmere and Coppell impressed me. He's quick, has good movement and a lot of courage. He can play on the right side, in the middle or with a roving commission. Given the right kind of club he has all it takes to be a very good player, a real proposition. He is a great player in the making, like Kevin Keegan in so many ways. If I was still at Liverpool, he would be in my team."

United scouts Jimmy Murphy and Johnny Carey both had a look at the 18-year-old winger and Tommy Docherty did the rest, signing him for £40,000 with another £20,000 to come after 20 League appearances.

Coppell joined United in March, 1975, just in time to help clinch promotion back to the First Division, and as The Doc said: "A team sometimes needs an injection of new blood and that was what Steve Coppell gave us after a spell of indifferent displays.

"As soon as he came in we started winning again. He is the kind of player who buzzes and this is infectious. A new player, if he is good enough, shakes people up and this is what Steve did for us. We got him as a prospect and he became a key figure in a great unbeaten run which saw us achieve promotion"

Then when Docherty took a chance on another winger from a lower division the following season, United really started to buzz. Coppell and Gordon Hill were wing specialists who blew the "wingless wonders" tactics of Sir Alf Ramsay out of the water. United finished third in the First Division and there was no looking back for Coppell as he went on to set a club record of 206 consecutive League appearances.

He was an FA Cup winner in 1977 and a few months later won the first of his 42 caps, no mean achievement for a player who had started out as a student part-timer in the Third Division.

Injury ended his career at the age of 28, but he was soon snapped up to become the League's youngest manager when he was appointed at Crystal Palace.

A former chairman of the PFA, he has also served as chief executive of the League Managers Association and returned briefly for an ill-fated stint as manager of Manchester City before returning to Palace.

PROFILE

BORN Croxteth, Liverpool
DATE OF BIRTH 9 July 1955
JOINED UNITED January 1974
FEE £60,000
PREVIOUS CLUB Tranmere
UNITED LEAGUE APPS 322
GOALS 54
INTERNATIONAL CAPS (England) 42
GOALS 7

> "He is the kind of player who buzzes and this is infectious."
>
> TOMMY DOCHERTY

ANDREW COLE

Andrew Cole has achieved more than most in football but he still struggles at times to please the critics.

PROFILE

BORN Nottingham
DATE OF BIRTH 15 October 1971
JOINED UNITED January 1995
FEE £7 million
PREVIOUS CLUBS Arsenal, Fulham (loan), Bristol City, Newcastle United
LEAGUE APPS 165
GOALS 80
INTERNATIONAL
CAPS (England) 13
GOALS 1

"I have just had to get on with it. I have always believed in my ability to score goals. I have taken a lot of flak, but fortunately the fans have been more loyal to me than some of the Press."

The player certainly has never forgotten the barb from Glenn Hoddle when he was England manager that he needs six chances before he scores, though it has to be said that he took his time before finding the net for the first time with England.

Controversy has dogged his career since joining Manchester United for £7m in January, 1995. Sir Alex Ferguson signed him in with great expectations after his scoring exploits for Newcastle which saw him run riot and score 68 goals in under two years.

But it proved a roller-coaster ride at Old Trafford, at first with injuries, including a broken leg and then illness, followed by a difficult partnership with Eric Cantona who was never slow to give Cole long meaningful looks whenever he failed to please him.

A lot of United fans blamed Cole for United missing out on the Championship in 1995 when he fluffed a number of scoring chances in a key match towards the end of the season against West Ham at Upton Park.

But he always retained the faith of the United manager and it wasn't long before he shrugged off all the criticism and roared back into top action . In season 1997-98 he suddenly caught fire with a hat-trick against Barnsley and a stunning three against Feyenoord in the European Champions League helping him to a purple patch of 11 goals in eight matches. It was United's first hat-trick in Europe for 30 years and bought him valuable time.

He finished the season with a total of 25 goals, easily the team's top scorer, and when Dwight Yorke arrived from Aston Villa, he struck up a magical partnership which saw the deadly duo shoot United to the 1999 treble of Premiership, FA Cup and the European Champions League.

Together in the League they scored a total of 53 goals with Cole hitting the winner against Spurs on the last day of the season to clinch the Premiership. He has coped well with the ups and downs of his career and as he says himself: "I have just had to get on with it. I have always believed in my ability to score goals. I have taken a lot of flak, but fortunately the fans have been more loyal to me than some of the Press."

Cole started his career as an apprentice with Arsenal but was farmed out on loan to Fulham and Bristol City before a £1.75m transfer to Newcastle in 1993. He helped Kevin Keegan's revival and set a Premiership scoring record with a total of 41 goals in his first season there, an achievement which brought him the PFA Young Player of the Year award.

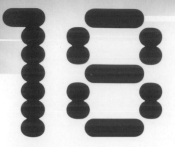

TOMMY TAYLOR

Sir Matt Busby lent his name to the youthful team he launched in the fifties in a football revolution that saw the Busby Babes start to sweep all before them.

PROFILE

BORN Barnsley
DATE OF BIRTH 29 January 1932
JOINED UNITED March 1953
FEE £29,999
PREVIOUS CLUB Barnsley
UNITED LEAGUE APPS 166
GOALS 112
INTERNATIONAL CAPS (England) 19
GOALS 16

"He was such a hot property that 20 clubs were said to be interested in him."

But though the manager believed in developing his own players, he had never been afraid to buy when he saw the need. The result was that in March, 1953, he paid £29,999 to bring Tommy Taylor from Barnsley to give his team a barnstorming centre forward.

The odd sum was an effort to avoid labelling the player with a £30,000 price tag, which was a lot of money in those days, though it failed to keep him out of the headlines because he was such an instant success. Anyone who scores twice on his debut, as Taylor did in a 5–2 win against Preston at Old Trafford, is more than halfway to getting the fans behind him, especially with the way he continued, picking up seven goals in the last remaining 11 League games of the season.

Taylor was a natural successor to Jack Rowley with his penetrating stride, fierce shooting and powerful heading.

His transfer from a struggling Second Division club to United, and the way he still delivered the goods in front of goal, immediately caught the eye of the England selectors and just two months after crossing the Pennines he won the first of his 19 England caps.

In all, he played 166 League games for United, scoring 112 goals, a ratio that has not been bettered. In 1955–56 he scored 25 goals from 33 appearances to make a vital contribution to United's Championship success, while on the European stage he had an incredible ratio of 11 goals from 14 starts. Even more importantly he had been the key link between Busby's first team built round players like Rowley and Stan Pearson and the newly emerging Babes.

United's biggest problem with Taylor had been to persuade him to leave Barnsley in the first place because he was happy in familiar surroundings. He was an unassuming lad and certainly gave Busby a fright when he was about to put pen to paper and said that there was still one thing worrying him.

United's officials waited with bated breath fearing a last-minute impossible demand, but all he wanted to know was if he would be able to get tickets for his parents to see him play!

That was hardly a problem after a chase for such a hot property that 20 clubs were said to be interested in him. In fact, Jimmy Murphy, United's assistant manager, said that the last time he saw Taylor play at Barnsley there were so many managers and chairmen there he thought it looked more like an extraordinary general meeting of the Football League!

Taylor had a mop of black hair and a perpetual smile on his face which prompted football writer George Follows to christen him "the smiling executioner."

Just as he had succeeded Rowley at club level, he proved the perfect follow-up for Nat Lofthouse in the England team. He played a leading role helping England qualify for the World Cup of 1958 in Sweden, but just as he missed the European Cup quarter-final second leg against Red Star Belgrade with United, he didn't live either to play in the World Cup that summer.

He lost his life in the Munich air crash at the age of 26, a career cut short but remembered vividly by those fortunate enough to have seen him play.

17 MARTIN BUCHAN

Martin Buchan was always that little bit different and independent, both on and off the field.

There was the time he refused to hand his passport back to the club because he considered he was quite capable of looking after it himself. It was Martin who turned up in collar and tie and blazer for a journey abroad when everyone else appeared in shorts and summer gear, even the manager, with the result that Martin Buchan looked more like the chairman than a player.

Asked by a reporter looking for an interview if he could have a quick word, Martin replied: "Certainly... velocity."

His independence showed at an early age when he went to a rugby-playing school in Aberdeen but refused to play the official sport and instead joined a Boys Brigade soccer team.

He says he wanted to be a professional footballer for as long he could remember, and when he was 17 Aberdeen invited him to join them full-time and follow in the footsteps of his father who had played at Pittodrie just after the war.

He was captain by the age of 21 and the youngest ever to skipper a club to victory in the Scottish Cup final at Hampden Park. The Scottish football writers voted him their Player of the Year, and it was not long before he won Scottish Under-23 and full caps.

Frank O'Farrell picked out the young central defender as the foundation for the rebuilding he knew had to be done when he became manager at Old Trafford and in March, 1972, he signed the guitar-playing Buchan for a then record £125,000.

O'Farrell was sacked after 18 months but he left a marvellous legacy in Buchan who went on to complete 11 seasons at Old Trafford. He played nearly 500 games to an impeccably high standard for three different managers, O'Farrell, Tommy Docherty and Ron Atkinson, and was captain for six years. He was demanding of both himself and those round him, once famously cuffing a wayward winger in his team, Gordon Hill, round the ear because he had, in his view as captain, failed to fulfil his defensive duties. He took United to Wembley three times and led the team to their notable FA Cup final victory over Liverpool in 1972.

In 1983 he moved on to Oldham but injury forced his retirement after just one season. He used to say that he didn't fancy management which would involve looking after awkward customers like himself. He tried it at Burnley but it was a short-lived attempt and he joined a sports manufacturer before later becoming an adviser with the PFA.

PROFILE

BORN Aberdeen
DATE OF BIRTH 6 March 1949
JOINED UNITED March 1972
FEE £125,000
PREVIOUS CLUBS Banks o'Dee, Aberdeen
UNITED LEAGUE APPS 376
GOALS 4

"Asked by a reporter looking for an interview if he could have a quick word, Martin replied: 'Certainly … velocity.'"

16 DENIS IRWIN

Denis Irwin marked St Patrick's Day, 2001, in a very special way. The quiet Irishman's appearance against Leicester City at Old Trafford was his 500th competitive game for Manchester United, taking in 350 League games, 43 in the FA Cup and 341 in the League Cup along with 65 outings in Europe.

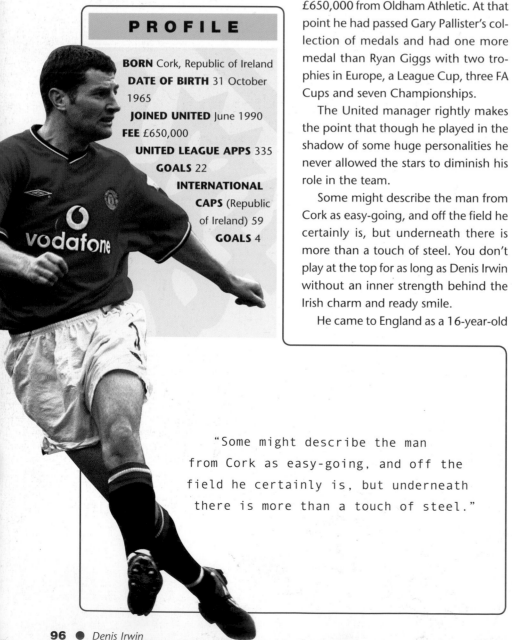

He joins Sir Bobby Charlton, Bill Foulkes, Alex Stepney, Tony Dunne and Joe Spence as United players who have reached the magic 500 and his achievement prompted Sir Alex Ferguson to say that Denis represented arguably the transfer bargain of his time as United manager after buying him for £650,000 from Oldham Athletic. At that point he had passed Gary Pallister's collection of medals and had one more medal than Ryan Giggs with two trophies in Europe, a League Cup, three FA Cups and seven Championships.

The United manager rightly makes the point that though he played in the shadow of some huge personalities he never allowed the stars to diminish his role in the team.

Some might describe the man from Cork as easy-going, and off the field he certainly is, but underneath there is more than a touch of steel. You don't play at the top for as long as Denis Irwin without an inner strength behind the Irish charm and ready smile.

He came to England as a 16-year-old to become an apprentice at Leeds United. He made 72 League appearances but at the end of season 1985–86 Billy Bremner gave him a free transfer. It was the lowest point of his career and he was ready to returen to Ireland when Oldham offered him a lifeline which he eagerly seized to spend four highly successful seasons at Boundary Park.

His career took another surprise twist on the back of two outstanding games playing for Oldham against United in the semi-final and replay of the FA Cup in 1990. Oldham lost the replay in injury time but Sir Alex Ferguson had liked the way the Irishman had stood up to his star-studded attack. He signed him at the end of the season and plunged him in at the deep end. Although he was moving up two divisions Denis settled quickly and helped win the European Cup Winners Cup. It was the start of United's glory charge with Denis switching uncomplainingly from left back to right and back again to accommodate other players.

Needless to say he was an outstanding international for the Republic, winning 59 caps before retiring from international football in January, 2000, at the age of 34 to extend his club life.

"I couldn't have wished to have been involved in a much better era for Irish football under Jack Charlton and Mick McCarthy. Playing Italy in the Giants Stadium in the World Cup of 1994 when we were the underdogs and beating them 1–0 was the highlight," he said.

PROFILE

BORN Cork, Republic of Ireland
DATE OF BIRTH 31 October 1965
JOINED UNITED June 1990
FEE £650,000
UNITED LEAGUE APPS 335
GOALS 22
INTERNATIONAL CAPS (Republic of Ireland) 59
GOALS 4

"Some might describe the man from Cork as easy-going, and off the field he certainly is, but underneath there is more than a touch of steel."

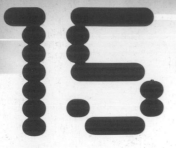

15 STEVE BRUCE

Steve Bruce wasn't Manchester United's first choice when Sir Alex Ferguson was looking round to rebuild his defence in the months following his arrival as manager in 1986.

He was trying to buy Terry Butcher from Glasgow Rangers until the England centre half broke his leg and he had an approach for Gary Pallister turned down by Middlesbrough.

But Norwich had been doing well and in December 1987, he decided to take a chance on the 27-year-old Bruce for £825,000 in what Ferguson would be the first to agree turned out to be a stunning piece of transfer business.

Nobody served Manchester United with more commitment. His cheerful personality and kind-hearted nature made him a popular figure and he was a natural choice to take over the captaincy from Bryan Robson.

He formed a partnership in central defence with Gary Pallister that must rank as one of the best in football. They defended brilliantly and appeared regularly together for several seasons with hardly a break. They would certainly have been worth trying as a pair for England, but though Pallister won international recognition, Steve Bruce remained arguably the best uncapped defender in the country. He was in at the start of Ferguson's drive for honours and played a major role in taking the club forward during his nine seasons at Old Trafford.

Who can forget, for instance, his dramatic intervention in the key League fixture a goal down against Sheffield Wednesday at Old Trafford with only four minutes to go?

Bruce left his defensive role to score twice, his second well into injury time, for a win which was probably the pivotal moment on their way to winning the Championship for the first time in 26 years. United had faltered the previous season, pipped by Leeds, but Bruce made it clear that this time there would be no wavering. It was a reflection of the whole-hearted attitude he brought to his game after an unpromising start in his native North East. He played for Wallsend Youth Club in Newcastle, along with Peter Beardsley, but while a number of his team-mates were taken on as juniors locally, Steve's only offer was from far-off Gillingham.

He made over 250 appearances for the Kent club, before a £135,000 move to Norwich where he helped them win promotion to the First Division and caught the eye of Manchester United.

He marked his United debut with a win against Portsmouth but also broke his nose and conceded a penalty. There were never any half measures with Steve who collected three Premiership titles with the distinction of two League and FA Cup doubles in three years.

He always insisted that he wanted to play for as long as possible, and when his regular first-team place looked under threat he joined Birmingham City in June 1996, on a free transfer to total more than 700 League appearances for his three clubs.

Since then he has managed at Sheffield United, Huddersfield and Wigan before his appointment to manage Crystal Palace.

PROFILE

BORN Corbridge, Northumberland

DATE OF BIRTH 31 December 1960

JOINED UNITED December 1987

FEE £825,000

PREVIOUS CLUBS Gillingham, Norwich City

UNITED LEAGUE APPS 325

GOALS 46

INTERNATIONAL CAPS (England) B team 1 (Captain)

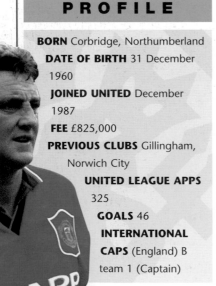

"The great thing about Steve is that he takes everything in his stride. He's a worker and a winner, just the type every team needs, and he had the strength of character to fit in straight away."

BRYAN ROBSON

"He's a real Manchester United player. Some strikers only dream of scoring as many goals as he does."

TOMMY DOCHERTY

NORMAN WHITESIDE

PROFILE

BORN Belfast
DATE OF BIRTH 7 May 1965
JOINED UNITED September 1978
FEE None
PREVIOUS CLUB Junior
UNITED LEAGUE APPS 212
GOALS 47
INTERNATIONAL CAPS (Northern Ireland) 38
GOALS 9

Norman Whiteside, a staunch Northern Irishman from the Shankhill Road area of Belfast, was discovered as a schoolboy player by Bob Bishop, United's scout in Northern Ireland, who was also responsible for sending George Best over to Old Trafford.

He was still a 17-year-old apprentice when Ron Atkinson gave him his League debut as a substitute at Brighton in April, 1982. A month later in the final game of the season he was in the starting line-up for a full debut and marked the occasion by scoring in a 2–0 win over Stoke City.

His impact was startling. Northern Ireland decided that if he was good enough for Manchester United he was good enough for them. They took him to the 1982 World Cup in Spain and gave him an international debut against Yugoslavia in Zaragoza to make him, at 17 years 41 days, the youngest ever World Cup player, younger even than Pele had been when he had arrived on the scene for Brazil.

Fans will remember for a long time his superbly struck shot which curled from a narrow angle round the goalkeeper to give United a 1–0 win over Everton in the 1985 FA Cup final at Wembley.

Sadly it was to prove his last notable achievement because the next three years saw him start to fight what became a losing battle against injuries.

He was sold to Everton in August 1989 for £750,000, but further injury forced him into retirement 15 months later. His career was over at the age of 26. As he says himself, "It was hard to take but there was no point sitting around looking for sympathy. So I went back to school."

He graduated in Sports Science at University College, Salford and is now a qualified podiatrist working for the Professional Footballers Association, screening young players for lower limb abnormalities. He is still in close touch with Old Trafford, working regularly on match days as a hospitality host.

Norman always complained that I wrote too much about his disciplinary record. But what alternative was there for a local team reporter who had watched Graeme Souness stretchered off after a Whiteside tackle; and who had seen him come on as a substitute against Liverpool to turn a 3-1 deficit into a draw with the help of flattening Steve McMahon, the player who had been terrorising United? I did in face admire his commitment as did Sir Alex Ferguson, which is why the manager forgave him his drinking problems towards the end of his time at Old Trafford.

"If Norman Whiteside had had one more yard of pace he would have been one of the greatest players ever produced in British football. But for continuous knee problems he would without doubt have become a truly world-class star. As it was he still managed to make a tremendous impact. He had incredible quality, an ice-cold temperament, wonderful vision and a good touch on the ball, all topped off with his famous aggressive streak."

SIR ALEX FERGUSON

13 JAAP STAM

Jaap Stam is a fierce looking character, big, shaven headed and not easily given to smiling, at least on the field of play. Perhaps it goes with his job as a top defender in the no-nonsense department of a team.

Looking at the Dutchman now, it is difficult to remember how he floundered in his first few games following his £10.75 million world record signing for a defender from PSV Eindhoven.

United fans remember his wobbles on his debut in the FA Charity Shield against Arsenal at the start of the 1998–99 season, and he hadn't been particularly impressive playing for Holland in the World Cup that summer.

Critics compared him with the outgoing Gary Pallister, forgetting completely of course that Pallister had struggled in his early days following his transfer from Middlesbrough.

What is beyond doubt now, though, is that the superb Stam quickly gave United a solidity at the back to compare with anything they have ever achieved in the past, and he did it despite being given a variety of partners.

At first it was with Gary Neville, then Ronnie Johnsen, David May, briefly Wes Brown, occasionally Henning Berg and then Mikael Silvestre. Eventually Brown and then Neville were brought back with Brown looking like his long-term partner. But despite the changes, Stam rarely faltered. He's outstanding in the air and tackles brilliantly; and when he goes forward the fans roar with excitement. There hasn't been a sight like that since big Gordon McQueen used to gallivant into the attack.

Stam made an amazing start to his United career in terms of trophies. To collect the Premiership, the FA Cup and European Championship in your very first season in a new country is Roy of the Rovers stuff.

Stam says: "I knew, as soon as I saw at first hand the strength of our squad and I looked through the side, that we could get to the final of the Champions League... and we did. I knew I was joining a big club with Manchester United but they are probably even bigger than I realised."

The unique treble seems to have whetted Stam's appetite for more.

"Some might have thought we would be bloated on our treble but we hardly talk about it in the dressing room. We all have our own special memories, but those ten glorious days in May of 1999 are now history," he explained. "Success can make players complacent. I have seen it happen but I know it won't at Manchester United. Sir Alex Ferguson has said he has a mechanism to detect if players are still hungry. I don't know what it is and I don't want to find out."

PROFILE

BORN Kampen, Holland
DATE OF BIRTH 17 July 1972
JOINED UNITED July 1998
FEE £10.75 million
PREVIOUS CLUBS
FC Zwolle,
Cambuur
Leeuwarden,
Willem 11,
PSV Eindhoven
UNITED LEAGUE APPS 63
GOALS 1
INTERNATIONAL CAPS (Holl) 39
GOALS 3

"Once Jaap has been here three or four years people will recognise him as one of the best defenders the club has ever had."
GARY NEVILLE

12 PAUL SCHOLES

I call him the Artful Dodger because nobody at Manchester United is more elusive than the ginger–haired Paul Scholes.

PROFILE

BORN Salford
DATE OF BIRTH 16 November 1974
JOINED UNITED July 1991
FEE None
PREVIOUS CLUB Junior
UNITED LEAGUE APPS 160
GOALS 41
INTERNATIONAL CAPS (England) 35
GOALS 13

"Paul Scholes is a lot of people's favourite footballer, and understandably so when you study the superb passing and wonderful vision he brings to his game in the middle of the park. I rate him one of the best finishers at the club and he always scores a good total of goals for a midfield player. He is rightly recognised by England as a reliable and first-rate performer."

Sir Alex Ferguson

It's a nickname that fits because not only is he hard to pin down on the pitch, he's just as hard to find off it!

He is a ball of action in his midfield role but once the game is over he disappears like a flash, heading back home to his house in Cheshire and his family. He hates interviews, doesn't have an agent and isn't interested in boosting his income with promotional and commercial work.

In fact when the club's own television station finally persuaded him to appear in front of their cameras they opened a bottle of champagne to celebrate the occasion!

The strange thing is that once you start chatting to the publicity-shy Paul, he talks easily and helpfully with a ready, bubbly laugh, though he still insists that he would much prefer to lead a quiet life away from television lights and reporters' notebooks.

But it is becoming increasingly more difficult for the local lad from nearby Salford to dodge the limelight as his fame as a footballer grows and he becomes more and more an important player for, not just Manchester United, but England.

For instance he certainly could not do much about the media interest which fell in on him like an avalanche when he scored a hat-trick for England against Poland at Wembley soon after Kevin Keegan had taken over from Glenn Hoddle as manager.

Keegan, naturally enough, became a firm favourite of the little guy and says "He's a fantastic player and because he plays with so many big names at Manchester United he is very underrated. Watching him in training you can see how much he loves his football and you should watch him in our shooting sessions. He certainly keeps the goalkeepers busy. He is a phenomenal trainer, a player who constantly impresses, and he can also play anywhere."

It was soon apparent when Sven Goran Eriksson took over from Keegan as England manager that he held the United midfielder in similar high regard and he quickly made him an integral part of his team.

Scholes still strives, though, to keep as low a profile as possible.

"I just don't enjoy interviews. They embarrass me. I suppose I get nervous. I hate talking about myself. I always run out of the back door at our training ground to avoid the Press. I jump into my car and drive off. I leave the interviewing to the other players," he explains.

"I like a quiet life. I don't drive a Ferrari, it's not my style, and in any case, it just wouldn't be practical these days as a family man. I don't have an agent and I don't want one. I don't want to go in front of cameras and all that stuff."

Scholes has a contract with United which runs until 2005 and he reckons he wants to stay at Old Trafford for the rest of his career.

"This is my home town and I never want to leave," he says.

11 MARK HUGHES

Sir Alex Ferguson describes Mark Hughes as "a warrior" and any study of the Welshman's approach to football offers ample evidence of why. His commitment to the cause made him a hero at Old Trafford, an admired player for Wales and appreciated abroad.

It was also the reason why Sir Alex brought him back from Barcelona and Bayern Munich for a second stint with Manchester United after growing up in Wrexham and starting his career at Old Trafford as a junior aged 16.

He forged a successful partnership with Norman Whiteside in the junior teams to help United reach the FA Youth Cup final for the first time for 18 years and won the PFA Young Player of the Year in 1985 when his international career started to blossom.

Capped by Wales at all levels, he struck a formidable strike partnership with Ian Rush to catch the eye of foreign clubs and in 1986 Barcelona came in for him. Hughes is the first to admit that going abroad was a mistake. He failed to hit it off with Gary Lineker and only began to prosper when the Spanish club sent him out on loan to Bayern Munich in Germany.

He once described his nightmare at the Nou Camp: "I was out of my depth, a mixed up lonely Welsh boy who didn't want to be there in the first place."

Sir Alex brought him home after two seasons abroad and said: "I felt it was a mistake for the club to have sold him in the first place... I have never seen a player with so much strength. He's really an awesome sight at close quarters."

The arrival of Eric Cantona signalled a potent partnership. Their goals were a telling factor at the start of United's trophy-winning run in the Nineties.

The man dubbed "Sparky" by his team-mates won two PFA Player of the Year awards and proved himself one of the most durable players in the game. For after what added up to 10 seasons with United, he set off on travels which took him first to Chelsea and then on to Southampton and Everton before signing for Blackburn Rovers to help them back into the Premiership.

Although he once told me he didn't think he would ever be interested in management, he became manager of Wales in 2000 and threw himself into the job with his usual commitment.

PROFILE

BORN Wrexham
DATE OF BIRTH 1 November 1963
JOINED UNITED June 1980
FEE None
PREVIOUS CLUB Junior
UNITED LEAGUE APPS 345
GOALS 119
INTERNATIONAL CAPS 65
GOALS 16

"On the pitch he was a devil. The more physical the battle the better he liked it. Off the pitch he was completely different, so shy, so quietly spoken. He wouldn't say boo to a goose and didn't seem the type to become a manager, but he is coping as manager of Wales so well that sooner or later he is going to be a big name in English football management."

ERIC HARRISON, HIS YOUTH TEAM COACH AT OLD TRAFFORD

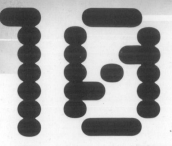

DENIS LAW

As far as United fans of the Sixties were concerned, Denis Law reigned as the King.

He was the people's champion as fans like the Stretford Enders found it easy to identify with a player whose aggression was so obvious.

The Lawman was slightly built, but there was a venom in his play which made him a hero and which at times could bring him into confrontation with opponents as well as referees.

It all added to his status and his followers liked the streak of villainy which ran through his football and which saw him serve two six-week suspensions in the course of his career. They loved his willingness to fly into the thick of the action with few holds barred.

Denis Law was daring, cocky, impudent and abrasive, which together with his lightning quick football, his flair for being in the right place at the right time, and his prolific goal scoring, was an explosive mix.

Bobby Charlton was admired, George Best was feted, but Law was worshipped because he brought together flair and fire. He flourished, especially in front of goal, where his scoring rate made him the most deadly marksman of all the famous players to perform on the Old Trafford stage.

Few from his era will forget the Law trademark as he signalled his goals to the crowd, punching the air and wheeling away with arm raised, his hand clutching his sleeve, save for the one finger pointing to the sky to acknowledge the strike. The terrace fans would rise to his salute as to a gladiator of old.

Yet few would have predicted a glittering career looking at Denis Law as a youngster, for he was under-sized and had a squint, but Bill Shankly took a chance on him at Huddersfield and he quickly showed he had other attributes to compensate for a lack of physique

He moved to Manchester City and then abroad to Torino before Matt Busby brought him home from Italy to flourish at Old Trafford. He was top scorer with 28 goals in the Championship season of 1964–65 and he top scored again with 23 when United won the League again two years later. He played his part getting there but was in hospital for a knee operation to miss the 1968 European Cup final.

He was voted European Footballer of the Year in 1964 and all Scots remember him with affection for his daring deeds in their international team. Readers of the *Scottish Daily Record* newspaper in 2001 voted him ahead of Kenny Dalglish and Jim Baxter as the greatest Scottish player of all time.

"He looked like a skinned rabbit. My first reaction was to say get him on the next train home."
BILL SHANKLY, HIS MANAGER AT HUDDERSFIELD.

"Denis Law was the most expensive signing I ever made, but on achievement he turned out to be the cheapest. Once we had got Denis to Old Trafford I knew we had the most exciting player in the game. He was the quickest thinking I ever saw, seconds quicker than anyone else. He had the most tremendous acceleration and could leap to enormous heights to head the ball with almost unbelievable accuracy, so often with the power of a shot."
SIR MATT BUSBY

"The strike partnership for Scotland of Denis Law and Kenny Dalglish was made in heaven."
SIR ALEX FERGUSON

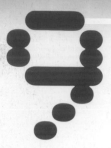

DUNCAN EDWARDS

Duncan Edwards admirers believe that if younger United fans had actually seen their hero play he would appear much higher than ninth in the voting for the Greatest players.

PROFILE

BORN Dudley, Worcs
DATE OF BIRTH 1 October 1936
JOINED UNITED June 1952
FEE None
PREVIOUS CLUB Junior
UNITED LEAGUE APPS 151
GOALS 20
INTERNATIONAL CAPS (England) 18
GOALS 5

To most supporters pre-Munich, Edwards was the greatest of them all. Certainly Jimmy Murphy, Sir Matt Busby's assistant believed so, and English football certainly lost an unbelievable talent when he died in a Munich hospital from the injuries he received in the United air crash of February 6th, 1958.

Duncan was only 21, but already he had more than made his mark with the promise of so much more to come for both Manchester United and England.

He had already won 18 caps when he lost his life and after captaining the England Schoolboy team and the Under-23 side, he was the natural successor to Billy Wright at senior level. He had been the youngest to play for England when he was given his first cap in April, 1955, at the age of 18 years and eight months, incidentally a debut marked by beating Scotland at Wembley 7-2.

United signed him from under the noses of Wolves, much to the annoyance of Stan Cullis, as a schoolboy and he soon stood out in the youth team, a boy who already looked a man with legs like tree trunks, a powerful chest and a tremendous zest for the game.

He was so good that he could play in any position. He was the youngest ever professional to appear in the First Division when United gave him his League debut against Cardiff City at Old Trafford on April 4th, 1953, at the tender ago of 16 and 185 days.

United lost 4-1 and he didn't play again that season, but the following year he strode majestically into action as Sir Matt Busby unveiled his Busby Babes.

He played superbly as the youthful Babes won the Championship in the successive years of 1956 and 1957. He scored in United's remarkable 5-4 First Division win at Arsenal just before the team flew out to Belgrade for their European Cup quarter-final against Red Star and the fateful refuelling stop at Munich on the way home.

It was tragically his last game on English soil.

"The greatest? There was only one, Duncan Edwards. If I shut my eyes I can see him now. Those pants hitched up, the wild leaps of boyish enthusiasm as he came running out of the tunnel, the tremendous power of his tackle – always fair but fearsome – the immense power on the ball. He played wing half, centre half, centre forward and inside forward with the consumate ease of a great player. He was quite simply a soccer Colosus."

THE LATE JIMMY MURPHY, UNITED'S ASSISTANT MANAGER

"Duncan had the promise of becoming the greatest of his day. He played with tremendous joy and his spirit stimulated the whole England team. It was in the character and spirit of Duncan Edwards that I saw the true revival of British football."

WALTER WINTERBOTTOM, HIS ENGLAND MANAGER

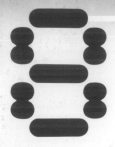

DAVID BECKHAM

David Beckham has become a cult player who has had to learn how to handle the sometimes conflicting life of sportsman and celebrity footballer, a situation made more glamorous and testing by his marriage to Spice Girl Victoria with her show-biz background.

Every facet of their lives is magnified by the media, and with every little thing blown up out of all proportion, Becks the footballer has handled his life well. Nobody has ever seriously doubted his application and commitment.

But stardom didn't come easily, and though he may now be the golden boy of English football, he has had to work hard to reach the top. In his early days he failed to win a place at the FA School of Excellence at Lilleshall, unlike his United team-mate, Andy Cole, and the England schoolboy selectors also turned him down as not big or strong enough. Perhaps that's why the boy concentrated on practising the skills which serve him so well today, and which now, harnessed to his more developed physique, make him such a phenomenal player.

He is, as Sir Alex Ferguson points out, the product of his own practice. It was his ball-juggling ability that contributed to one of the most significant moments of his young career. David had long been a United fan, encouraged by his parents, who despite living near London in Tottenham Hotspur's recruiting area, had always been United followers and visitors to Old Trafford when they could manage it.

One day in 1986 he saw Bobby Charlton's soccer school advertising a skills competition. He entered and, aged 11, emerged the star pupil to win the first prize of a week training with the Barcelona youth team in Spain.

From then on United had their eye on him and he signed schoolboy forms for them on his 14th birthday. He joined as a trainee in 1991 and a year later he was starring in the side that won the FA Youth Cup.

He made his League debut early the next season and since then has been swept along as part of United's trophy-winning team, making particularly important contributions in the final stages of winning the unique treble in 1999 when he switched into a central midfield role. The question of which is his best position, in midfield, or on the right wing with his raking crosses, is an on-going debate.

His international career has kept pace with his success at club level – the high spot undoubtedly being asked to captain England in 2001 by new manager, Sven-Göran Eriksson. But he has had his problems with England, too, with fans from other clubs abusing not just him but Victoria and his son, Brooklyn.

His popularity dipped when he was sent off playing against Argentina at the 1998 World Cup in France when his dismissal turned him into the scapegoat for England's exit from the tournament.

But he fought his way back and remains a staunch United man who seems likely to sign a new contract when his present agreement runs out in 2002.

PROFILE

BORN Leytonstone
DATE OF BIRTH 2 May 1975
JOINED UNITED July 1991
FEE None
PREVIOUS CLUBS Junior
UNITED LEAGUE APPS 175
GOALS 36
INTERNATIONAL CAPS (England) 42
GOALS 4

"David is the best player in the world. He is under double the pressure that I have to face. He is a great guy, too. He deserves to be European Footballer of the Year."

ALESSANDRO DEL PIERO OF JUVENTUS

"He has the best stamina of any player at the club. He's a great player with an incredible appetite and when you have ability harnessed to work-rate, you cannot ask for anything more."

SIR ALEX FERGUSON

ROY KEANE

Nobody is more popular at Old Trafford than Roy Keane. You have only to listen to the chant of "Keano" rolling round the ground to know that while the fans may also love their more dazzling, attacking stars, the captain is the man at the core of their support.

He has matured a great deal since his early tempestuous days with Nottingham Forest after joining Brian Clough from Cobh Ramblers, in the Republic of Ireland, for a modest £10,000 aged 19.

Even his early days with United following a then English record transfer of £3.75m in July, 1993, were periodically disrupted with wild moments but by his own admission he has quietened down, both on and off the field, as perhaps befits a family man with three children.

He demonstrated his desire for a settled life when he signed a new contract in December, 1999, to stay with United for a further four years rather than seek a bigger fortune abroad. He admitted that one of the reasons for turning his back on Italy was that he didn't fancy leaving his two dogs in quarantine for six months. So much for the hard man.

At the same time, inside the shaven headed Keane, is still a tough guy capable of frightening the strongest... as photographs showed only too clearly when he went wild with referee Andy D'Urso for awarding a controversial penalty against United in a match against Middlesbrough at Old Trafford.

Sir Alex Ferguson took Keane to task for that excess, but of course it is the passion and commitment, burning deep inside him and evidenced in his all-action style of play, that so endears him to the United following.

It was undoubtedly his fierce determination which enabled him to return to action better than ever despite missing virtually the whole of season 1997–98 following a serious injury with ruptured cruciate ligaments.

Keane has the admiration of his manager as well as the fans. The player has a hunger to match his own and Ferguson knows that, despite the intoxicating trophy treble success of 1999, Keane will maintain his edge and ambition.

The Irishman says so himself and reveals a contempt for players who settle for less. As he puts it: "Once you stop to think of what you have achieved you start worrying. That was a problem here before all the success of the 1990s. Too many players were happy just to play for United. They won the odd cup in the 80s, but that's not enough. At United you must aim for the League, world championships and European trophies."

He expects those around him to be similarly driven and upset his team-mates at the end of season 2000-01 when he accused them of letting success go to their heads.

He claimed that despite winning the championship for the third successive year, the Champions League quarter-final defeat against Bayern Munich showed them they are only an average team and perhaps the time had come for new faces.

Shortly afterwards, his improved discipline evaporated with a shocking foul on Manchester City captain Alfie Haaland to bring him his eighth dismissal in eight years at Old Trafford.

PROFILE

BORN Cork, Republic of Ireland
DATE OF BIRTH 10 August 1971
JOINED UNITED July 1993
FEE £3.75m
PREVIOUS CLUBS Cobh Ramblers, Nottingham Forest
UNITED LEAGUE APPS 185
GOALS 24
INTERNATIONAL CAPS (Republic of Ireland) 52
GOALS 8

"I see him as the heartbeat of Manchester United."
SIR ALEX FERGUSON

"Ask any United player who means the most to the team and they would say Roy Keane. He is all talents rolled into one."
NORMAN WHITESIDE

BRYAN ROBSON

Bryan Robson was so much the outstanding player of his era in the Eighties that United at times were tagged a one-man team.

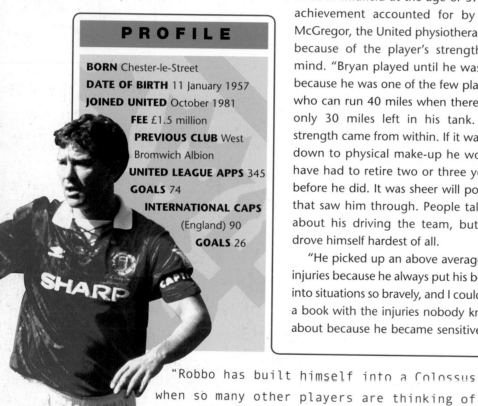

Not for nothing was he known as Captain Marvel and certainly he was missed during his absences through injury which lengthened as he grew older. In fact one analyst examined the performances of the team with and without Robson and found that his presence made a difference of 20 points a season.

Robson played for 13 years at Old Trafford and was still a potent driving force in midfield at the age of 37, an achievement accounted for by Jim McGregor, the United physiotherapist, because of the player's strength of mind. "Bryan played until he was 37 because he was one of the few players who can run 40 miles when there are only 30 miles left in his tank. His strength came from within. If it was all down to physical make-up he would have had to retire two or three years before he did. It was sheer will power that saw him through. People talked about his driving the team, but he drove himself hardest of all.

"He picked up an above average of injuries because he always put his body into situations so bravely, and I could fill a book with the injuries nobody knew about because he became sensitive to admitting he had been hurt again," hr explained.

His fortitude revealed itself early because after leaving his native North East to become an apprentice with West Bromwich Albion he had to overcome breaking one leg twice and soon afterwards breaking the other one.

He forced himself to make the grade and the first move made by Ron Atkinson when he became manager of United in 1981 was to go back to his old club and buy Robson for £1.5m.

He gave great service and along the way turned down a lucrative transfer to Italy in order to stay in Manchester. He became an inspiration for England as well as United, winning 90 caps and scoring 26 goals.

The sad part was that he didn't play in particularly successful times for either club or country and certainly one wonders what he might have achieved if he had been in his prime for Sir Alex Ferguson. He helped win the FA Cup three times, but the Championship eluded him until his final season when he made 17 League appearances, most of them as a substitute, finally to bring the League title to Old Trafford after a 26-year absence. I suspect the cheers were as much for Robson as the trophy when he and Steve Bruce jointly held the Championship Cup aloft in May 1993, before leaving to become player-manager of Middlesbrough.

Twice he brought Middlesbrough back into the Premiership, and though with the help of Terry Venables he staved off relegation last season, he was sacked to make way for Steve McClaren.

PROFILE

BORN Chester-le-Street
DATE OF BIRTH 11 January 1957
JOINED UNITED October 1981
FEE £1.5 million
PREVIOUS CLUB West Bromwich Albion
UNITED LEAGUE APPS 345
GOALS 74
INTERNATIONAL CAPS (England) 90
GOALS 26

"Robbo has built himself into a Colossus when so many other players are thinking of chucking their boots into the corner cupboard for good."
RON ATKINSON TALKING ABOUT HIS CAPTAIN AT THE AGE OF 32

"When the flak flies a lot of people keep their heads down, but when the call came to stand up and be counted our captain did exactly that."
ENGLAND MANAGER BOBBY ROBSON
AFTER THE 1988 EUROPEAN CHAMPIONSHIPS

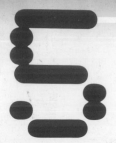

PETER SCHMEICHEL

Peter Schmeichel's statistics of 292 League appearances tell only half the story of his eight seasons in goal for Manchester United.

The Great Dane, as he became known in popular headlines, was a commanding figure who played a major part in the team's prize-winning run in the Nineties culminating in the treble in 1999 before setting off for a new life with Sporting Lisbon in Portugal.

United first noticed him when they were in Spain on a winter break. Brondby were staying in the same hotel. The two teams shared a training pitch and because Sir Alex Ferguson had been told about this goalkeeper breaking through in Danish football he stopped behind one day to watch him.

His enthusiasm and fanaticism in training, as well as his obvious competence, immediately impressed the United manager, and though Brondby turned down their first approach United went back as his contract began to run out to strike a deal at £505,000.

The son of a Polish musician who emigrated to Denmark, his father wanted him to be a pianist but football called. As a boy he was a United fan who trained wearing a Gary Bailey replica kit.

With his skills honed by United, he returned to Denmark to become a hero by helping them become the 1992 European Champions, his high point a penalty save against Marco van Basten to put the Danes through to a final against Germany which they won 2–0.

Back at Old Trafford he became a dominating character who was outstanding in one-on-one situations, spreading himself to pull off seemingly impossible saves. He guarded his goal with a fierceness felt by his own defenders as well as opponents as he shouted and waved his arms at Gary Pallister and Steve Bruce who explained: "Peter craved perfection so much he would rant and rave if he had a shot to save but it was his way of maintaining his concentration. We always had a drink afterwards."

United fans will never forget his last game and the way he left his post in injury time of the European Champions League final in Barcelona to join the rest of the team in the Bayern Munich goal-mouth for the last-chance corner kicks.

He undoubtedly distracted the Germans as Teddy Sheringham and Ole Solskjaer rammed home the goals for victory in what was a fitting climax to a great United career.

"He blossomed into the best goalkeeper Manchester United have ever had and the best I have worked with. He ranks up there with Gordon Banks, Peter Shilton, Lev Yashin and all the other outstanding keepers. He is brave, quick and has a massive presence. He has been a model professional who has inspired us all on his way to becoming one of the most influential players in arguably the most successful period in the club's history."

SIR ALEX FERGUSON

"Winning the Portuguese Championship meant a lot to me because not only have I won the League in every country I have played in, Denmark, England and now Portugal, but because I felt I was being written off at the end of my time with United and I have proved them wrong."

PETER SCHMEICHEL

SIR BOBBY CHARLTON

Bobby Charlton running in full stride, cheeks puffed out with the effort, and unleashing one of his thunderous shots, was one of the most stunning sights in English football.

PROFILE

BORN Ashington, Northumberland
DATE OF BIRTH 11 October 1937
JOINED UNITED January 1953
FEE None
PREVIOUS CLUB Junior
UNITED LEAGUE APPS 606)
GOALS 199
INTERNATIONAL CAPS (England) 106
GOALS 49

When he was in full flow for goal, there was a grace and beauty about him, a balletic quality, which singled him out as one of the most distinctive players in the game's history. What also made him special was that he had a sporting spirit which saw him commit only one disciplinary offence in the whole of his career, a booking for failing to retreat at a free kick which was subsequently wiped off his record by the Football Association as a mistake!

He was an idol without feet of clay, a gentleman and a sportsman supreme whose behaviour was exemplary both on and off the field. He retired from football in 1973 and 11 years later became a director of Manchester United, a position he still holds along with many others as a football consultant and sporting ambassador who was knighted in 1994.

Signed as a schoolboy from the North East, United gave him his League debut against Charlton Athletic at Old Trafford on 6 October 1956, but only 14 months later he was caught up in the Munich air crash. Goalkeeper Harry Gregg dragged him clear of the wreckage and after a few weeks' recuperation he was able to start playing again.

Charlton threw himself into the game, and in season 1958–59, he played 38 League games and scored 28 goals. He helped to beat Leicester to win the FA Cup in 1963, and was a key figure in the Championship success of 1965.

It was at this stage that his international career reached a peak. He had made his England debut a few months after the Munich accident, playing against Scotland, and over the next 12 years he won 106 caps while scoring 49 goals, a record which still stands.

His great year came in 1966 when two typical Charlton goals against Portugal, fierce shots, which gave the goalkeeper no chance, put England through to the final of the World Cup and victory against Germany, sharing the Wembley pitch with his brother Jack.

He was voted Footballer of the Year by England's soccer writers, followed by European Footballer of the Year, as well as the referees' award as a Model Player.

Bobby Charlton was in his pomp with Championship medals in 1965 and 1967 before sharing in United's great European Cup triumph of 1968 when he scored twice against Benfica in the final at Wembley.

In all he played First Division football for 17 seasons to total a club record of 604 appearances and score a record 199 goals.

> "When things looked their blackest after the Munich accident, and there were times when I felt great despair, I was enormously cheered to think that Bobby Charlton was there. His presence was a great source of inspiration to keep working for the restoration of Manchester United."
>
> SIR MATT BUSBY

> "His high standard of behaviour on stage still remains an example and a reproach to others … a mirror of deeper values."
>
> GEOFFREY GREEN OF THE TIMES

RYAN GIGGS

There is no more thrilling sight than Ryan Giggs flying down the left wing with the ball seemingly tied to his boot laces.

PROFILE

BORN Cardiff

DATE OF BIRTH 29 November 1973

JOINED UNITED July 1990

FEE None

PREVIOUS CLUBS Junior

UNITED LEAGUE APPS 290

GOALS 59

INTERNATIONAL CAPS (Wales) 32

GOALS 7

Cup in a semi-final replay at Villa Park in 1999. He ran from the halfway line in a mazy dribble which seemed to take him through the entire Gunners' defence to score what has been described as the Goal of the Century.

He had spent the first hour on the bench because of a tight hamstring which has plagued him in recent seasons. It may also explain why in some respects he was overtaken by David Beckham as the star attacking turn and number one pin-up boy.

> "I know how good he is because I have to play against him in training every week...To me he is the best left winger in the world... Giggsy has just got everything. He is brave, he is elusive, he is quick and he works hard.He has got a different level of stamina to everyone else at the club... If Giggsy decides he wants to go full out, he just breezes past you. It is almost like he is taking the mickey."
>
> TEAM-MATE GARY NEVILLE

Visions of George Best and Bobby Charlton easily come to mind, as they did when he scored his memorable goal to knock Arsenal out of the FA

The recurring injury has been a worry, though there was no doubt about the impact he made when he first burst on to the scene in 1991 and was voted Young Player of the Year at the end of his first full season, an honour to be repeated two years later.

With his coal-black eyes and dark curly hair he was an appealing figure for the media as well as a precocious talent, a kind of Ryan's Express providing penetration and pace down the left flank.

He has worked hard to overcome his nagging injury problems which cast him in a bad light in Wales because of the number of times he was forced to pull out of international matches.

"Every day both before and after training I do special exercises to work on my hamstrings, the worst kind of injury for a quick player like me who likes to run at defenders with the ball at my feet and make sudden changes of direction as well as trying to accelerate. When you are flying you become fearless. I was like that when I first came into the side as a teenager and the main thing is to become consistent," he explained.

Giggs has made well over 300 appearances for United now and only Denis Irwin of his contemporaries has made more. With 10 years' service behind him and a testimonial coming up, he says: "I am a Manchester United fan first and foremost. Ever since I came here we have always been winning things and as long as that continues there would be no point in going anywhere else. I'm happy here."

His parents are Welsh but he captained the England Boys team because he grew up in Salford. He was Ryan Wilson then, the son of Danny Wilson, a Welsh international Rugby League player who played in the Manchester area. After his parents split up he changed to his mother's maiden name of Giggs. Manchester City had their eye on him but United stepped in to bring him to Old Trafford as a schoolboy.

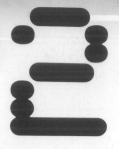

GEORGE BEST

George Best lived life in the fast lane on and off the field, and at the height of his powers, was as devastating as a footballer as he was later as a cult figure.

PROFILE

BORN Belfast

DATE OF BIRTH 22 May 1946

JOINED UNITED August, 1961

FEE None

PREVIOUS CLUBS United junior

UNITED LEAGUE APPS 361

GOALS 137

INTERNATIONAL CAPS (Northern Ireland) 37

GOALS 9

"He has tremendous temperament, no situation is bigger than him. He can rise to any level and with experience he will be a giant."
SIR MATT BUSBY AT THE OUTSET OF GEORGE BEST'S CAREER

"George Best was the greatest player in the world."
PELE

For this essentially shy Irishman was a truly gifted player while at the same time becoming a popular icon taking soccer into a more glamorous world.

His talent was the key of course, but he also had a good-looking magnetism which saw him admired by men and yearned for by girls. All over the country they gazed at him through the windows of the team bus waiting to leave after a match. Not that he paid much attention because invariably waiting for him at home would be a succession of Miss Worlds and Miss Great Britains!

He tuned football into the Swinging Sixties, a trendy dresser who launched his own boutique as well as his own night club which he called Slack Alice.

Some say Slack Alice got her man early because he was only 26 when he turned his back on Manchester United and his lifestyle towards the end of his playing career certainly caught up with him in later life.

Drink and a damaged liver have become a problem which has seen him spend increasingly more time living in his native Northern Ireland, though still returning regularly to his home in London for his role as a soccer pundit with Sky television. In demand as a guest speaker, and as newsworthy as ever, his popularity seems unwavering, a measure of the impact he made as a young man. I watched him blossom into a rare per-former who in my view still stands alone as the most extraordinary, exhilarating player I have even seen.

I never found it difficult to forgive him his early departure from Old Trafford because in my view George Best more than paid his dues to the game. He might have left it young, but he started young and played for 11 seasons in the First Division. By the time he quit Old Trafford he had played 466 League, Cup and European games and scored 178 goals.

The other significant fact is that once he had established himself in the side he rarely missed a game. In six of his seasons he made either 40, 41 or an ever-present 42 League appearances each year. That's hardly the career of a fly-by-night.

The highlight of his career was undoubtedly winning the European Cup in 1968. It was George who produced the inspired moment against Benfica in the final at Wembley. The game had gone into extra time at 1–1 and it was George who broke Benfica with a superb goal to set his team on their way to a 4–1 triumph. It was his best-ever scoring year with 28 League goals from 41 appearances. George was voted Player of the Year in Northern Ireland. The English writers gave him their award as well and he was voted European Footballer of the Year, the youngest ever.

The following season was the beginning of the end. Busby retired and successive managers found George increasingly difficult to manage. So it all ended in tears as George slid down the slippery slope to play for Hibs, Dunstable, Stockport County, Fulham and in America.

But what great memories he left behind!

ERIC CANTONA

Eric Cantona holds a special place in the hearts of Manchester United supporters. The fans hailed him as le Dieu, the god who led their team to the promised land of the Championship after 26 long, frustrating years without winning the League.

As soon as he started playing for United midway through season 1992-93 the team was transformed and lost only twice after Christmas on their way to the title. Sir Alex Ferguson had found the perfect catalyst for his young players as well as a striker who could change the course of a game on his own with a touch of magic or a goal.

The fairy tale lasted until May 1997, when the great man vanished from Old Trafford almost as suddenly as he had arrived from Leeds.

The arrogant strut and familiar turned-up collar will never be forgotten in Manchester. Nor will his beautiful football, the telling pass, the vision, the masterly goals and all the other superb touches which contributed so much to the four Premiership titles and two FA Cup wins United enjoyed during his four and a half years at Old Trafford.

Cantona was 31 when he left Manchester, eventually settling in Barcelona after retiring from all but beach football and trying his hand as an actor.

A maverick as well as a fantastic player, he arrived at the right club, at the right time, to work for the right manager, surrounded by the right players.

He had been a professional for nearly nine years and his career had gone nowhere significant except to achieve notoriety as the enfant terrible of French football. He had virtually had to flee his own country in order to find a club willing to take him on and even in England it had proved difficult.

It hadn't worked out at Sheffield Wednesday where he had had a brief trial and despite helping Leeds United with the Championship, manager Howard Wilkinson clearly didn't rate his contribution very highly or he would not have passed him on to Alex Ferguson for a give-away million!

At Old Trafford though, everything fell into place and Cantona found a manager who understood him, an essential element in his story because he still had some bizarre moments of ill-discipline.

Even Ferguson thought it would be impossible for him to resume his career in England after his notorious kung-fu attack on a Crystal Palace spectator at Selhurst Park in January 1995, but when the player expressed interest in staying Ferguson supported him. It was a remarkable act of faith by Ferguson in the face of hysterical clamour, and the manager was rewarded by watching the player contribute to winning two more Championships involving a second League and Cup double to ensure his place among the Old Trafford legends.

Now supporters hope that the suggestion that he might return to take guest coaching sessions with United's youngsters will prove true.

PROFILE

BORN Marseille, France
DATE OF BIRTH 24 May 1966
JOINED UNITED November 1992
FEE £1.2 million
PREVIOUS CLUBS Auxerre (twice), Marigues, Olympique Marseille (twice), bordeaux, Montpellier, Nîmes, Sheffield Wednesday (loan), Leeds United
UNITED LEAGUE APPEARANCES 106 (1)
GOALS 53
INTERNATIONAL CAPS 45
INTERNATIONAL GOALS 14

"Eric graced our stage splendidly. It was a pleasure just to watch him training and he undoubtedly raised the awareness of our young players at the time. Old Trafford was his spiritual home for nearly five years. He was blessed with a special talent and I was delighted when he came back to play in the Munich Memorial match at Old Trafford in 1998 to say a proper farewell to his adoring fans."

SIR ALEX FERGUSON

PICTURE CREDITS

The publishers would like to thank the following for their kind permission to reproduce the pictures in this book:

Action images: 9, 10, 13, 21, 37, 46, 66, 95, 120, 125

Allsport: 16, 45, 54, 72, 101

Colorsport: 8, 12, 25, 27, 29, 36, 40, 41, 44, 57, 61, 68, 69, 70, 71, 73, 75, 78, 88, 89, 92, 93, 100, 109, 110, 111, 124

Empics: 3, 18, 19, 22, 28, 31, 35, 39, 47, 50, 63, 65, 74, 121, 126, 127, 128

Hulton Archive: 33, 38, 42, 43, 49, 52, 59, 60, 64, 67, 77, 94

John & Matthew Peters/Manchester United FC: 11, 15, 26, 34, 55, 56, 58, 76, 79, 82, 83, 84, 85, 86, 87, 90 , 91, 96, 97, 98, 99, 102, 103, 104, 105, 106, 107, 112, 113, 114, 115, 116, 117, 118, 119, 122, 123

Mark Leech: 23, 53

MSI: 14, 17, 24, 30, 32, 80, 108

Popperfoto: 20, 48, 51, 62, 81

Rex: 6

Every effort has been made to acknowledge correctly and contact the source and/or copyright holder of each picture, and Carlton Books Limited apologises for any unintentional errors or omissions which will be corrected in future editions of this book.